Carrying on in Key Stage 1

Providing continuity in purposeful play and exp

Sculpting, Stuffing and Squeezing

Ros Bayley, Lynn Broadbent, Sally Featherstone

C000082635

Reprinted 2009
Published 2008 by A&C Black Publishers Limited
36 Soho Square, London W1D 3QY
www.acblack.com

ISBN 978-1-906029-12-8

First published 2008 by Featherstone Education Limited

Text © Ros Bayley, Lyn Broadbent, Sally Featherstone 2008
Illustrations © Kerry Ingham 2008
Photographs © Lynn Broadbent, Ros Bayley,
Sally Featherstone, Sarah Featherstone 2008

A CIP record for this publication is available from the British Library.

All rights reserved. No part of this publication may be reproduced
in any form or by any means - graphic, electronic, or mechanical, including
photocopying, recording, taping or information storage or retrieval systems -
without the prior permission in writing of the publishers.

Printed in Malta by Gutenberg Press Ltd

This book is produced using paper that is made from wood grown in
managed, sustainable forests. It is natural, renewable and recyclable.
The logging and manufacturing processes conform to the environmental
regulations of the country of origin.

To see our full range of titles

visit www.acblack.com

Contents

	Page
Introduction	4
The Role of the Adult	5
Looking for the Learning	6
Taking it Further	7
Programme of Study for Key Stage 1; photocopiable grid	8
Clay	9-12
Mud and Compost	13-16
Dough	17-20
Wire	21-24
Paper Pulp	25-28
Ice	29-32
Plaster and Plaster Bandages	33-36
Balsa Wood and Sandpaper	37-40
Wax and Soap carving	41-44
Shaving Foam and Spray Cream	45-48
Fruit and Vegetables	49-52
Stuffing	53-56
Moulding	57-60
Fabric	61-64
Combined Materials	65-68
Programme of Study for Key Stage 1 (abbreviated version)	69-74
Websites and resources	75-76

Introduction

This series of books is intended to support the continuing growth and development of independent learning and practical activities, which are key features of the Early Years Foundation Stage (EYFS).

Children in Key Stage One need and deserve the chance to **build on the best of practice in the EYFS**, which carefully balances adult directed tasks with learning that children initiate and develop themselves, often in the company of responsive adults. These activities, which include sand and water play, construction, role play, independent mark making and writing, creative work, dance and movement, and outdoor play, are some of the activities children value most and miss most in Years One and Two.

> Parent: 'What's it like in Year 1?'
>
> Child: 'There en't no sand and the work's too 'ard.'

This quote from a Year 1 boy echoes the feelings of many children who need to continue the learning styles and situations offered in Reception classes. However, many teachers in Key Stage One feel intense pressure to concentrate on activities that require recording and increasing levels of direction by adults. Why is this, and is it right for teachers to feel so pressured?

One thing we know from research is that **practical activity and independent learning are essential for brain growth** and reinforcement of growing abilities throughout childhood, at least until the onset of puberty, and for many children this is a lifelong need. We also know that the embedding of learning and the transformation of this into real understanding takes time and practice. Skills need to be reinforced by revisiting them in many different contexts in child-initiated learning, and practical challenges, and practical tasks in real life situations will be far more effective than rote learning, worksheets or adult direction.

> 'I hear and I forget,
>
> I see and I remember,
>
> I do and I understand.'
>
> Ancient Chinese Proverb

It is also clear from brain research that **many boys (and some girls) are just not ready by the end of Reception to embark on a formal curriculum** which involves a lot of sitting down, listening and writing. Their bodies and their brains still need action, challenge and freedom to explore materials and resources in freedom.

But this does not mean that challenge should be absent from such activity! The brain feeds on challenge and novelty, so teachers and other adults working in Key Stage One need to structure the experiences, so they build on existing skills and previous activities, while presenting new opportunities to explore familiar materials in new and exciting ways. Such challenges and activities can:

- 🔥 be led by the Programme of Study for Key Stage One;
- 🔥 focus on thinking skills and personal capabilities;
- 🔥 relate to real world situations and stimuli;
- 🔥 help children to achieve the five outcomes for *Every Child Matters*.

EVERY CHILD MATTERS
The five outcomes:
Enjoy and achieve
Stay safe
Be healthy
Make a positive contribution
Achieve economic well-being

In **Carrying on in Key Stage 1**, we aim to give you the rationale, the process and the confidence to continue a practical, child-centred curriculum which also helps you as teachers to recognise the requirements of the **statutory curriculum for Key Stage One**. Each book in the series follows the same format, and addresses objectives from many areas of the National Curriculum. Of course, when children work on practical challenges, curriculum elements become intertwined, and many will be going on simultaneously.

The Role of the Adult

Of course, even during child initiated learning, **the role of the adult is crucial**. Sensitive adults play many roles as they support, challenge and engage the children in their care. High quality teaching is not easy! If teachers want to expand experiences and enhance learning, they need to be able to stand back, to work alongside, <u>and</u> extend or scaffold the children's learning by offering provocations and challenges to their thinking and activity. The diagram below attempts to describe this complex task, and the way that adults move around the elements in the circle of learning. For ease of reading we have described the elements in the following way, and each double page spread covers all three of the vital roles adults play.

Recognising and building on the practical activities which children have experienced before

This element of the process is vital in scaffolding children's learning so it makes sense to them. Your knowledge of the Foundation Stage curriculum and the way it is organised will be vital in knowing where to start. Teachers and other adults should have first hand knowledge of both the resources and the activities which have been available and how they have been offered in both child-initiated and adult-led activities. This knowledge should be gained by visiting the Reception classes in action, and by talking to adults and children as they work. Looking at Reception planning will also help.

Understanding the range of adult roles, and the effect different roles have on children's learning

Responsive adults react in different ways to what they see and hear during the day. This knowledge will influence the way they plan for further experiences which meet emerging needs and build on individual interests. The diagram illustrates the complex and interlinking ways in which adults interact with children's learning. Observing, co-playing and extending learning often happen simultaneously, flexibly and sometime unconsciously. It is only when we reflect on our work with children that we realise what a complex and skilled activity is going on.

Offering challenges and provocations

As the adults collect information about the learning, they begin to see how they can help children to extend and scaffold their thinking and learning. The adults offer challenges or provocations which act like grit in an oyster, provoking the children to produce responses and think in new ways about what they know and can do.

Linking the learning with the skills and content of the curriculum

As the children grapple with new concepts and skills, adults can make direct links with curriculum intentions and content. These links can be mapped out across the range of knowledge, skills and understanding contained in the curriculum guidance for Key Stage One. It is also possible to map the development of thinking skills, personal capabilities and concepts which link the taught curriculum with the real world.

The adult as extender of learning
discusses ideas
shares thinking
makes new possibilities evident
instigates new opportunities for learning
extends and builds on learning and interests
supports children in making links in learning
models new skills and techniques

The adult as co-player
shares responsibility with the child
offers suggestions
asks open questions
responds sensitively
models and imitates
plays alongside

The adult as observer
listens attentively
observes carefully
records professionally
interprets skilfully

Looking for the Learning

As children plan, explore, invent, extend, construct, discuss, question and predict in the rich experiences planned and offered, they will communicate what they are learning through speech and actions, as well as through the outcomes of activities. **Assessment for learning** involves adults and children in discussing and analysing what they discover. Reflecting on learning, through discussion with other children and adults, is a key factor in securing skills and abilities, fixing and 'hard wiring' the learning in each child's brain. And, of course, teachers and other adults need to **recognise, confirm and record children's achievements**, both for the self esteem this brings to the children and to fulfil their own duties as educators.

You could find out what children already know and have experienced by:

* talking to them as individuals and in small groups;

* talking to parents and other adults who know them well (teaching assistants are often wonderful sources of information about individual children);

* visiting the Reception classes and looking at spaces, storage and access to resources, including the use of these out of doors;

* providing free access to materials and equipment and watching how children use them when you are not giving any guidance;

* talking as a group or class about what children already know about the materials and those they particularly enjoy using.

Using the curriculum grid to observe, to recognise learning and celebrate achievement

At the end of each section you will find a curriculum grid which covers the whole Programme of Study for Key Stage 1. This is a 'shorthand version' of the full grid included at the end of the book on pages 69-74. A black and white photocopiable version of the grid appears on page 8, so you can make your own copies for planning and particularly for recording observations.

We suggest that as the children work on the provocations and other challenges in this book, adults (teachers and teaching assistants) can use the grid to observe groups of children and record the areas of the curriculum they are covering in their work. The grids can also be used to record what children say and describe in plenary sessions and other discussions.

These observations will enable you to recognise the learning that happens as children explore the materials and engage with the challenging questions you ask and the problems you pose. And of course, as you observe, you will begin to see what needs to happen next; identifying the next steps in learning! This logical and vital stage in the process may identify:

* some children who will be ready for more of the same activity;

* some who need to repeat and reinforce previous stages;

* some who need to relate skills to new contexts, the same activity or skill practised in a new place or situation;

* some who will want to extend or sustain the current activity in time, space or detail;

* others who will wish to record their work in photos, drawings, models, stories, video and so on.

Critical and Thinking Skills

The grid also identifies the key skills which children need for thinking about and evaluating their work. Many schools now observe and evaluate how well these skills are developing when children work on challenging projects and investigations.

Taking it further

Offering extension activities is a way of scaffolding children's learning, taking the known into the unknown, the familiar into the new, the secure into the challenging. It is the role of the adult to turn their knowledge of the children into worthwhile, long-term lines of enquiry and development which will become self-sustaining and last throughout life.

At the end of each section in the book you will find a selection of useful resources, links and other information to help you bring construction to life. You could use these resources by encouraging individuals and groups:

* to **use the Internet** to find images and information;

* to **use ICT equipment** such as cameras, tape recorders, video and dictaphones to record their explorations and experiments;

* to **explore information books** in libraries and other places at home and at school;

* to **make contact by email and letter** with experts, craftsmen, artists, manufacturers, suppliers and other contacts;

* to **make books, films, PowerPoint presentations**;

* to **record their work** in photographs and other media;

* to **respond to stimuli** such as photographs, video, exhibitions and other creative stimuli;

* to **look at the built and natural environment** with curiosity, interest and creativity;

* to **become involved in preserving the natural world**, develop environmental awareness and support recycling;

* to **look at the world of work** and extend their ideas of what they might become and how they might live their lives;

* to **develop a sense of economic awareness** and the world of work in its widest sense;

* to **feel a sense of community** and to explore how they might make a contribution to the school and wider communities in which they live;

* to **work together and develop the ability to think, reason and solve problems** in their learning.

We recommend that younger children should always work with an adult when accessing search engines and Internet sites.

The suggested resources include websites, books, contacts and addresses. There are also some photographs which may inspire young learners as they work on the provocations and challenges suggested.

We hope you will find the ideas in this book useful in stimulating your work with children in Year 1 and Year 2. Before trying the activities please check for allergies and be aware of safety at all times. The ideas, photos and provocations we have included are only a start to your thinking and exploring together, of course you and the children will have many more as you start to expand the work they do in these practical areas, providing a rich curriculum base using familiar and well loved materials.

Ros Bayley, Lynn Broadbent, Sally Featherstone: 2008

Observation of _____ (the activity and resources)

Literacy

	Lit 1 speak	Lit 2 listen	Lit 3 group	Lit 4 drama	Lit 5 word	Lit 6 spell	Lit 7 text1	Lit 8 text2	Lit 9 text3	Lit10 text4	Lit11 sentence	Lit12 present-ation
Literacy	1.1	2.1	3.1	4.1	5.1	6.1	7.1	8.1	9.1	10.1	11.1	12.1
	1.2	2.2	3.2	4.2	5.2	6.2	7.2	8.2	9.2	10.2	11.2	12.2

Numeracy

	Num 1 U&A	Num 2 count	Num 3 number	Num 4 calculate	Num 5 shape	Num 6 measure	Num 7 data
Numeracy	1.1	2.1	3.1	4.1	5.1	6.1	7.1
	1.2	2.2	3.2	4.2	5.2	6.2	7.2

Date	
Names	

Science

	SC1 Enquiry			SC2 Life processes					SC3 Materials		SC4 Phys processes		
	Sc1.1	Sc1.2	Sc1.3	Sc2.1	Sc2.2	Sc2.3	Sc2.4	Sc2.5	Sc3.1	Sc3.2	Sc4.1	Sc4.2	Sc4.3
Science	1.1a	1.2a	1.3a	2.1a	2.2a	2.3a	2.4a	2.5a	3.1a	3.2a	4.1a	4.2a	4.3a
	1.1b	1.2b	1.3b	2.1b	2.2b	2.3b	2.4b	2.5b	3.1b	3.2b	4.1b	4.2b	4.3b
	1.1c	1.2c	1.3c	2.1c	2.2c	2.3c		2.5c	3.1c		4.1c	4.2c	4.3c
	1.1d				2.2d				3.1d				4.3d
					2.2e								
					2.2f								
					2.2g								

ICT

	ICT 1 finding out	ICT 2 ideas	ICT 3 reviewing	ICT 4 breadth
ICT	1.1a	1.2a 2a	3a	4a
	1.1b	1.2b 2b	3b	4b
	1.1c	`1.2c 2c	3c	4c
		1.2d		

History

	H1 chronology	H2 events, people	H3 inter-pret	H4 enquire	H5 org & comm	H6 breadth
History	1a	2a	3a	4a	5a	6a
	1b	2b		4b		6b
						6c
						6d

Geography

	G1.1 & G1.2 enquiry		G2 places	G3 processes	G4 environment	G5 breadth
Geography	1.1a	1.2a	2a	3a	4a	5a
	1.1b	1.2b	2b	3b	4b	5b
	1.1c	1.2c	2c			5c
	1.1d	1.2d	2d			5d
			2e			

PE

	PE1 devel skills	PE2 apply skills	PE3 evaluate	PE4 fitness	PE5 breadth
PE	1a	2a	3a	4a	5a dance
	1b	2b	3b	4b	5b games
		2c	3c		5c gym

Art & Design

	A&D1 ideas	A&D2 making	A&D3 evaluating	A&D4 materials	A&D5 breadth
Art & Design	1a	2a	3a	4a	5a
	1b	2b	3b	4b	5b
		2c		4c	5c
					5d

PHSE & C

	PSHEC1 conf & resp	PSHEC2 citizenship	PSHEC3 health	PSHEC4 relationships
PHSE & C	1a	2a	3a	4a
	1b	2b	3b	4b
	1c	2c	3c	4c
	1d	2d	3d	4d
	1e	2e	3e	4e
		2f	3f	
		2g	3g	
		2h		

D&T

	D&T 1 developing	D&T 2 tool use	D&T 3 evaluating	D&T 4 materials	D&T 5 breadth
D&T	1a	2a	3a	4a	5a
	1b	2b	3b	4b	5b
	1c	2c			5c
	1d	2d			
	1e	2e			

Music

	M1 performing	M2 composing	M3 appraising	M4 listening	M5 breadth
Music	1a	2a	3a	4a	5a
	1b	2b	3b	4b	5b
	1c			4c	5c
					5d

Key to KS1 PoS on Pages 69-74

Critical Skills	Thinking Skills
problem solving	observing
decision making	classifying
critical thinking	prediction
creative thinking	making inferences
communication	problem solving
organisation	drawing conclusions
management	
leadership	

Notes on how to take the learning forward:

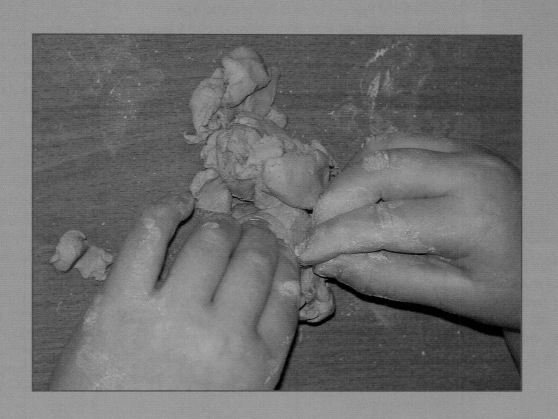

Clay

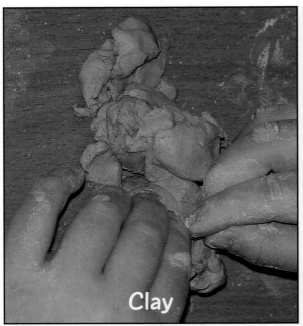

Clay

Previous experience in the Foundation Stage

Many settings use clay as an additional material, as it has properties unlike any other malleable material. However, some settings will have avoided it for various reasons. Those children who have had access to clay may have:

* used it in free play;
* rolled coils for constructions;
* used clay in role play and home corner play as 'pretend' objects and food;
* made simple models and shapes.

Others may not have had any experience of clay and may need encouragement to address its challenges as well as experiencing its unique properties.

Pause for thought

In the early stages of working with clay it is crucial to continue to observe the children. Only by doing this can you set developmentally appropriate challenges and provocations. The ideas listed here are offered as suggestions; the most exciting challenges will arise from children's own interests and motivations, which will only become apparent as you spend time with them, watching and joining them in their play. As you do this, you will be moving between the three interconnecting roles of observer, co-player, extender described below, and will be able to decide what you need to do next to take the learning forward.

The responsive adult (see page 5)

In three interconnecting roles, the responsive adult will be:

* observing
* listening
* interpreting

observer

* **modelling**
* **playing alongside**
* **offering suggestions**
* **responding sensitively**
* **initiating with care!**

co-player

* discussing ideas
* sharing thinking
* modelling new skills
* asking open questions
* being an informed extender
* instigating ideas and thoughts
* supporting children as they make links in learning
* making possibilities evident
* introducing new ideas and resources
* offering challenges and provocations

extender

Offering challenges and provocations - some ideas:

You may choose to use clay that does not need firing (eg Newclay). or potter's clay which either needs firing in a kiln or recognising its shortcomings. Painting any clay with PVA glue will lengthen its life, even though it may not prevent breaking. Whichever type you choose to offer, children need periods of free play before addressing any challenges. Clay also needs to be kept damp!

? Can you use clay to make long 'sausages' or 'snakes'? Who can make the longest? Now coil your snakes and make them into flat mats or tiles. You can smooth our the joins or leave them as a decoration. What happens to your clay as it dries?

? Get some rolling pins and roll some clay until it is flat. Cut some squares or other shapes with a knife. Now decorate your clay tiles with patterns, pictures or writing, using old pencils, sticks or twigs from the garden.

? Some animals are good to make with clay - choose ones with shorter legs and fatter bodies, such as hedgehogs. Make a list of the animals you could try (use a book or Google to help you). Now make some animals from the list - use tools such as pencils or scissors to make fur and feather patterns, or stick natural materials such as feathers or leaves. When your animals are finished, you could fire them in a kiln, or cover them with a layer of PVA glue.

? Use some flat clay to take prints. Roll the clay out, press natural objects into the surface, leave the clay for a while, then paint the surface. How can you turn this into a print on paper or fabric?

? Make some very runny clay by adding lots of water and stirring it up. Use this clay as paint or ink to draw or write on paper with paint brushes. What happens of you paint all over the paper and leave it to dry? How could you use it now?

Ready for more?

- Try doing some cave paintings. Get some clay and make it very runny by mixing with water. Put it in several pots and colour the different pots with some of these natural dyes:
  - turmeric (a yellow spice)
  - blackberry or blueberry juice
  - charcoal or soot

  Now use your paints to paint on card, paper, or even a wall. Look at the great images of cave paintings on Google Images 'cave paintings'.
- Use clay to make hand prints. Make blocks as big as your hand and press your hand into the block. Get your friends to do the same. What do you find out?
- Make lots of balls of clay. Can you use these to make a sculpture?
- Get some wire netting. Make it into a structure and cover it with clay. How did you do it?
- Look up 'terracotta army' in Google Images. These soldiers were found in China. Can you find out how many there are? Could you make a terracotta soldier?
- Use Google Images to find pictures of terra cotta sculptures of your favourite animals. Why is this sort of sculpture called terracotta? How do you cook clay?

Materials, equipment suppliers, websites, books and other references

Clay is a cheap and versatile natural material. There are lots of different sorts, and you may want to offer a choice of types or colours:

* grey or buff clay is a school standard, clean and easy to use. Get this from your school supplier or consortium;

* terra cotta or red clay is the most authentic, but it does stain hands and other surfaces;

* Newclay or self-hardening clay is useful as the fibres within the clay can be hardened with a special hardener, so creations don't need firing - see http://www.newclay.co.uk/Products.htm for newclay products and other clays.

* If you live or work on clay soil, you could help the children to dig their own clay direct from the ground.

www.commotionstore.co.uk - for clay tools

Visit your local museum or art gallery, or look in *Yellow Pages* for sculptors and potters in your area who may be prepared to visit you or open their studio for a visit.

For inspiration for creations, use **Google Images** 'sculpture' 'clay model' 'animal sculpture' or any animal eg 'cat sculpture'

Some **websites**:

www.warriortours.com/.../xian/0010656.htm - to look at the Terracotta army

http://www.schoolsliaison.org.uk/kids/greecepot.htm Birmingham Museum children's site

http://www.gladstone.stoke.gov.uk/ccm/portal/ Stoke on Trent Museum service for visits to the Potteries.

'museum pottery kids' in a search engine such as google will find lots of museums with facilities for schools.

There are hundreds of books on using clay and making sculptures. Here are just a few **books** for younger readers:

Fun with Modeling Clay; Barbara Reid; Kids Can Press
Ceramics for Kids; Mary Ellis; Lark Books
Clay in the Primary School; Peter Clough; A&C Black
The Great Clay Adventure: Creative Handbuilding Projects for Young Artists; Ellen Kong; Davis Publications
Children, Clay and Sculpture; Cathy Weisman Topal; Davis Publications
Exploring Clay with Children: 20 Simple Projects; Chris Utley; A&C Black

Curriculum coverage grid overleaf

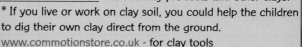
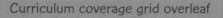

Potential NC KS1 curriculum coverage through the provocations suggested for clay.

Literacy	Lit 1 speak	Lit 2 listen	Lit 3 group	Lit 4 drama	Lit 5 word	Lit 6 spell	Lit 7 text1	Lit 8 text2	Lit 9 text3	Lit10 text4	Lit11 sentence	Lit12 presentation
	1.1	2.1	3.1	4.1	5.1	6.1	7.1	8.1	9.1	10.1	11.1	12.1
	1.2	2.2	3.2	4.2	5.2	6.2	7.2	8.2	9.2	10.2	11.2	12.2

Numeracy	Num 1 U&A	Num 2 count	Num 3 number	Num 4 calculate	Num 5 shape	Num 6 measure	Num 7 data
	1.1	2.1	3.1	4.1	5.1	6.1	7.1
	1.2	2.2	3.2	4.2	5.2	6.2	7.2

Science	SC1 Enquiry			SC2 Life processes					SC3 Materials		SC4 Phys processes		
	Sc1.1	Sc1.2	Sc1.3	Sc2.1	Sc2.2	Sc2.3	Sc2.4	Sc2.5	Sc3.1	Sc3.2	Sc4.1	Sc4.2	Sc4.3
	1.1a	1.2a	1.3a	2.1a	2.2a	2.3a	2.4a	2.5a	3.1a	3.2a	4.1a	4.2a	4.3a
	1.1b	1.2b	1.3b	2.1b	2.2b	2.3b	2.4b	2.5b	3.1b	3.2b	4.1b	4.2b	4.3b
	1.1c	1.2c	1.3c	2.1c	2.2c	2.3c		2.5c	3.1c		4.1c	4.2c	4.3c
	1.1d				2.2d				3.1d				4.3d
					2.2e								
					2.2f								
					2.2g								

ICT	ICT 1 finding out		ICT 2 ideas	ICT 3 reviewing	ICT 4 breadth
	1.1a	1.2a	2a	3a	4a
	1.1b	1.2b	2b	3b	4b
	1.1c	1.2c		3c	4c
		1.2d			

Full version of KS1 PoS on pages 69-74
Photocopiable version on page 8

D&T	D&T 1 developing	D&T 2 tool use	D&T 3 evaluating	D&T 4 materials	D&T 5 breadth
	1a	2a	3a	4a	5a
	1b	2b	3b	4b	5b
	1c	2c			5c
	1d	2d			
	1e	2e			

History	H1 chronology	H2 events, people	H3 interpret	H4 enquire	H5 org & comm	H6 breadth
	1a	2a	3a	4a	5a	6a
	1b	2b		4b		6b
						6c
						6d

Geography	G1.1 & G1.2 enquiry		G2 places	G3 processes	G4 environment	G5 breadth
	1.1a	1.2a	2a	3a	4a	5a
	1.1b	1.2b	2b	3b	4b	5b
	1.1c	1.2c	2c			5c
	1.1d	1.2d	2d			5d
			2e			

Music	M1 performing	M2 composing	M3 appraising	M4 listening	M5 breadth
	1a	2a	3a	4a	5a
	1b	2b	3b	4b	5b
	1c			4c	5c
					5d

PHSE & C	PSHEC1 conf & resp	PSHEC2 citizenship	PSHEC3 health	PSHEC4 relationships
	1a	2a	3a	4a
	1b	2b	3b	4b
	1c	2c	3c	4c
	1d	2d	3d	4d
	1e	2e	3e	4e
		2f	3f	
		2g	3g	
		2h		

Art & Design	A&D1 ideas	A&D2 making	A&D3 evaluating	A&D4 materials	A&D5 breadth
	1a	2a	3a	4a	5a
	1b	2b	3b	4b	5b
		2c		4c	5c
					5d

PE	PE1 devel skills	PE2 apply skills	PE3 evaluate	PE4 fitness	PE5 breadth
	1a	2a	3a	4a	5a dance
	1b	2b	3b	4b	5b games
		2c	3c		5c gym

Critical skills	Thinking Skills
problem solving	observing
decision making	classifying
critical thinking	prediction
creative thinking	making inferences
communication	problem solving
organisation	drawing conclusions
management	
leadership	

Mud and Compost

Mud and Compost

Previous experience in the Foundation Stage

Mud and compost are free resources for all schools, and are now a feature of most early years settings. The majority of children will have experimented with and explored these resources in:

* making mud pies;
* working with mud in a builder's tray, with diggers, small world figures and vehicles, making miniature gardens;
* playing in a digging area, with and without tools, burying objects in mud and digging them up again;
* planting and gardening in pots and in the ground;
* paddling in muddy puddles;
* mixing water with mud for painting.

Pause for thought

In the early stages of working with these materials it is crucial to continue to observe the children. Only by doing this can you set developmentally appropriate challenges and provocations. The ideas listed here are offered as suggestions; the most exciting challenges will arise from children's own interests and motivations, which will only become apparent as you spend time with them, watching and joining them in their play. As you do this, you will be moving between the three interconnecting roles of observer, co-player, extender described below, and will be able to decide what you need to do next to take the learning forward.

The responsive adult (see page 5)

In three interconnecting roles, the responsive adult will be:

observer

* observing
* listening
* interpreting

co-player

* **modelling**
* **playing alongside**
* **offering suggestions**
* **responding sensitively**
* **initiating with care!**

extender

* discussing ideas
* sharing thinking
* modelling new skills
* asking open questions
* being an informed extender
* instigating ideas and thoughts
* supporting children as they make links in learning
* making possibilities evident
* introducing new ideas and resources
* offering challenges and provocations

Offering challenges and provocations - some ideas:

Some children (and adults) need to get used to using mud and compost. If the children are not used to these media, give them time to experiment, or provide some simple tools.

? Can you find some mud that can be easily moulded? Try digging mud from different places to see which is most malleable.

? Can you change the colour of mud by adding different substances to it, for example, powder or ready-mixed paint, food colouring?

? Can you change the consistency of mud by adding things like water, wallpaper paste, sand or flour?

? Can you make a castle, or other type of building from mud? What could you use to make turrets and towers? Can you make bridges from mud?

? Make a cave from mud, and use some small world fantasy characters to make stories and plays.

? Can you create a habitat for small world animals?

? Can you construct some bowls and find ways of drying them out so that they do not break? Can you stop them breaking by mixing other things with the mud?

? Can you make your own bricks and then design some buildings that you could make using your own bricks?

? Can you make a tunnel with mud? Who can make the longest tunnel? Can you find ways of reinforcing your tunnel to make it stronger?

? How could you make a sculpture of a person or animal from mud? Which animals are easy to make? Is it harder to make a person sculpture or an animal sculpture?

? Can you make some decorative mud pies? How many different materials can you find for decorating them, for example, flowers, feathers, leaves, shells and stones?

? Take photographs of your mud pies and use them to make a decorative picture, book or wall hanging.

Ready for more?

- Google 'mud sculptures' to see if you can find different ways of working with mud.

- Can you make a mythical beast, dragon or similar creature? You may need to use other materials such as twigs or sticks to help support your sculpture.

- Can you combine other materials with mud, for example, straw or newspaper to make 'cob' houses or other structures? Look on Google Images for 'cob cottages' for some information.

- Make some mud casts of handprints, footprints and other objects which leave impressions in mud. Once they are dry, fill them with plaster of Paris. Look for some footprints or animal prints around the school grounds or gardens. Try making mud casts of these and finding out what made them.

- Can you create a 'living sculpture' by adding seeds and plants to your sculpture? For example, sow grass seeds to make 'hair' or mustard and cress seeds for fur.

- Try making some tiles with your mud, by flattening it and cutting the tiles out. Look for some pictures of mosaics and decorate or colour your tiles to make your own mosaic?

- Experiment with sieves and colanders to strain the water from mud for your sculptures.

Materials, equipment suppliers, websites, books and other references

Mud is free, but if children are going to use their hands, it should be collected from places where it has not been fouled by animals. If you don't have access to clean earth, buy a bag of compost from a garden centre.

Any tools will do for work with mud:
- small sized gardening tools
- old spoons, forks and blunt knives
- yogurt pots and other recycled materials
- sticks, twigs and other found objects.

Google Images 'mud sculpture' for a great hippo sculpture 'mud sculpture kids' 'cob cottage' for buildings covered in mud 'mud bricks'.

http://www.pbase.com/qleap/mud for some great pictures of children in the Arizona Mud Mania. Go to the home page and click on each year for a gallery of photos. Google web 'fun with mud' will give you lots of sites with mud races and mud festivals.

'I am Clay' is an American DVD for teachers about the benefits of clay work. Watch a preview with some good ideas, or order the video on http://k-play.com/I_am_clay.html - there is a gallery on the same site with examples of children's work from a range of ages.

http://www.iamanartist.ie/clay/ has a slide show and lots of ideas - just click on the drawings.

Some suitable **books** for younger readers include:

Mudworks; MaryAnn F. Kohl; Bright Ring Publishing

Mud Pies and Other Recipes: A Cookbook for Dolls; Marjorie Winslow; Walker & Company

Mud Pie Annie; Sue Buchanan; ZonderKidz

Stuck in the Mud; Jane Clarke; Puffin Books

Making Art with Sand and Earth; Gillian Chapman; PowerKids Press

Let's Make Mud! Gwenda Turner; Penguin Books NZ

Mud, Grass, and Ice Homes (Homes Around the World); Debbie Gallagher; Smart Apple Media

Mud Puddle; Robert N. Munsch; Annick Press

The Mud Monster; Rosemary Billam; Franklin Watts

Stuck in the Mud; Shirley Jackson; Ladybird

Curriculum coverage grid overleaf

Potential NC KS1 curriculum coverage through the provocations suggested for mud and compost.

Full version of KS1 PoS on pages 69-74
Photocopiable version on page 8

Literacy

Lit 1 speak	Lit 2 listen	Lit 3 group	Lit 4 drama	Lit 5 word	Lit 6 spell	Lit 7 text1	Lit 8 text2	Lit 9 text3	Lit10 text4	Lit11 sentence	Lit12 presentation
1.1	2.1	3.1	4.1	5.1	6.1	7.1	8.1	9.1	10.1	11.1	12.1
1.2	2.2	3.2	4.2	5.2	6.2	7.2	8.2	9.2	10.2	11.2	12.2

Numeracy

Num 1 U&A	Num 2 count	Num 3 number	Num 4 calculate	Num 5 shape	Num 6 measure	Num 7 data
1.1	2.1	3.1	4.1	5.1	6.1	7.1
1.2	2.2	3.2	4.2	5.2	6.2	7.2

Science

SC1 Enquiry			SC2 Life processes					SC3 Materials		SC4 Phys processes		
Sc1.1	Sc1.2	Sc1.3	Sc2.1	Sc2.2	Sc2.3	Sc2.4	Sc2.5	Sc3.1	Sc3.2	Sc4.1	Sc4.2	Sc4.3
1.1a	1.2a	1.3a	2.1a	2.2a	2.3a	2.4a	2.5a	3.1a	3.2a	4.1a	4.2a	4.3a
1.1b	1.2b	1.3b	2.1b	2.2b	2.3b	2.4b	2.5b	3.1b	3.2b	4.1b	4.2b	4.3b
1.1c	1.2c	1.3c	2.1c	2.2c	2.3c		2.5c	3.1c		4.1c	4.2c	4.3c
1.1d				2.2d				3.1d				4.3d
				2.2e								
				2.2f								
				2.2g								

ICT

ICT 1 finding out		ICT 2 ideas	ICT 3 reviewing	ICT 4 breadth
1.1a	1.2a	2a	3a	4a
1.1b	1.2b	2b	3b	4b
1.1c	1.2c		3c	4c
	1.2d			

D&T

D&T 1 developing	D&T 2 tool use	D&T 3 evaluating	D&T 4 materials	D&T 5 breadth
1a	2a	3a	4a	5a
1b	2b	3b	4b	5b
1c	2c			5c
1d	2d			
1e	2e			

History

H1 chronology	H2 events, people	H3 interpret	H4 enquire	H5 org & comm	H6 breadth
1a	2a	3a	4a	5a	6a
1b	2b		4b		6b
					6c
					6d

Geography

G1.1 & G1.2 enquiry		G2 places	G3 processes	G4 environment	G5 breadth
1.1a	1.2a	2a	3a	4a	5a
1.1b	1.2b	2b	3b	4b	5b
1.1c	1.2c	2c			5c
1.1d	1.2d	2d			5d
		2e			

Music

M1 performing	M2 composing	M3 appraising	M4 listening	M5 breadth
1a	2a	3a	4a	5a
1b	2b	3b	4b	5b
1c			4c	5c
				5d

PHSE & C

PSHEC1 conf & resp	PSHEC2 citizenship	PSHEC3 health	PSHEC4 relationships
1a	2a	3a	4a
1b	2b	3b	4b
1c	2c	3c	4c
1d	2d	3d	4d
1e	2e	3e	4e
	2f	3f	
	2g	3g	
	2h		

Art & Design

A&D1 ideas	A&D2 making	A&D3 evaluating	A&D4 materials	A&D5 breadth
1a	2a	3a	4a	5a
1b	2b	3b	4b	5b
	2c		4c	5c
				5d

PE

PE1 devel skills	PE2 apply skills	PE3 evaluate	PE4 fitness	PE5 breadth
1a	2a	3a	4a	5a dance
1b	2b	3b	4b	5b games
	2c	3c		5c gym

Critical skills	Thinking Skills
problem solving	observing
decision making	classifying
critical thinking	prediction
creative thinking	making inferences
communication	problem solving
organisation	drawing conclusions
management	
leadership	

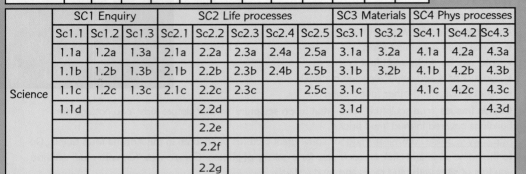

Dough

Dough

Previous experience in the Foundation Stage

By the time children leave the Foundation Stage they should have had wide experience of using dough in projects and particularly in free play:

* indoors and out of doors;
* to make role play objects;
* with small world animals and figures;
* to explore pattern and shape in three dimensions;
* for strengthening hands and fingers;
* exploring dough mixed with sand, glitter, perfumed oils and other substances;
* to make models and familiar objects.

They should also have had experience of:

* working on specific projects with dough in language and mathematical activities.

Pause for thought

In the early stages of working with these materials it is crucial to continue to observe the children. Only by doing this can you set developmentally appropriate challenges and provocations. The ideas listed here are offered as suggestions; the most exciting challenges will arise from children's own interests and motivations, which will only become apparent as you spend time with them, watching and joining them in their play. As you do this, you will be moving between the three interconnecting roles of observer, co-player, extender described below, and will be able to decide what you need to do next to take the learning forward.

The responsive adult (see page 5)

In three interconnecting roles, the responsive adult will be:

* observing
* listening
* interpreting

observer

* **modelling**
* **playing alongside**
* **offering suggestions**
* **responding sensitively**
* **initiating with care!**

co-player

* discussing ideas
* sharing thinking
* modelling new skills
* asking open questions
* being an informed extender
* instigating ideas & thoughts
* supporting children as they make links in learning
* making possibilities evident
* introducing new ideas and resources
* offering challenges and provocations

extender

Offering challenges and provocations - some ideas:

It is important to find out the breadth of experience children have had during the EYFS, particularly in using dough for projects. You may also want to explore making your own dough with the children.

? Get a copy of *The Little Book of Dough* (from Featherstone Education). This book has a huge range of recipes for making dough, using different sorts of materials and additions.

? Try making your own dough, using the *Little Book* or a recipe from the Internet. Find out what this dough can do, and take some photos.

? Can you make coloured dough? What could you use? You could try natural colourings like beetroot juice, onion skins or grated carrot.

? Can you make perfumed dough? What could you use? Look for food flavourings as well as perfumes.

? Can you make a big structure with dough? Try making lots of balls and using these to build with. Can you make a tower? A bridge? A wall?

? Make some dough that can be hardened in the oven or on a radiator. Roll some out and use objects to press in and make patterns on the dough. Make a hole with a pencil, so you can hang your decoration up. Wait until your decorations are dry, colour them with pens or paint, or just paint them with a mixture of white glue and water to stop them breaking.

? Make some edible dough and use this to make shaped or decorative biscuits or cookies, or decorate them with edible decorations when they are cooked. You could sell your biscuits to other children or take them home for your family to eat.

Ready for more?

🥄 Make some dough and colour it if you wish. Use the dough to make bricks, then bake these until they are hard. Use your bricks to make structures and buildings. You can stick them together with glue, clay or uncooked dough.

🥄 Use the internet, cookery books and craft books to make two lists of all the things you can use to make dough. You could list edible/not edible, cooked/not cooked, easy/difficult, cheap/expensive. Now choose some ingredients to make some dough yourself.

🥄 Can you think of any more ingredients that you could use to make dough? Try some. Did it work?

🥄 Make some dough that can be hardened in an oven. Colour it if you like, then use this dough to make some badges or fridge magnets. Roll the dough out and cut out small shapes. Decorate these with letters, marks, patterns, or press small objects into them (make sure these can be baked!). Bake the shapes on a baking sheet, then paint or colour them. Stick a magnet or a badge pin on the back. You could make these for your friends.

🥄 Find out how to make dough from cotton wool or the fluff from tumble driers. Make some and see what it is like. Can you make dough with coffee or chocolate?

Materials, equipment suppliers, websites, books and other references

There are hundreds of different recipes for dough, and many can be made by the children independently. Put 'dough recipe' in a search engine to come up with lots of ideas. Look on USA and worldwide sites as well, as these sometimes have unusual versions. Ask your local shops for flour that is past its 'sell by date' to use in dough recipes.

Educational suppliers all have a range of tools and other equipment for dough work - try www.tts-group.co.uk www.ascoeducational.co.uk or **your local consortium group**. Look in Bargain and 'pound' shops for cutters and shaping tools, and encourage children to be inventive in the tools they make or the objects they use.

Don't forget edible doughs for making biscuits and cookies, and try some of the doughs with more unusual ingredients such as:

* chocolate
* freezer dough
* tumble drier fluff
* cotton wool
* couscous
* mashed potato
* sand.

Of course, not all of these are edible!

See lots of lovely pictures of dough creations on **Google** 'dough sculpture' 'dough sculpture kids'.

Look on **Google Images** 'dough' 'playdough' 'kids dough' 'salt dough' 'dough recipes'.

http://www.multihobbies.com/saltdough/ has dough recipe and a gallery of dough creations.

Some suitable **books** for younger readers include:
Salt Dough Models; Sue Organ; Search Press
The Little Book of Dough; Lynn Garner; Featherstone Education
Salt Dough; Laura Torres; American Girl
Salt Dough Fun; Brigitte Casagranda; Gareth Stevens

Curriculum coverage grid overleaf

Potential NC KS1 Curriculum Coverage through the provocations suggested for dough.

Full version of KS1 PoS on pages 69-74
Photocopiable version on page 8

Literacy

	Lit 1 speak	Lit 2 listen	Lit 3 group	Lit 4 drama	Lit 5 word	Lit 6 spell	Lit 7 text1	Lit 8 text2	Lit 9 text3	Lit10 text4	Lit11 sentence	Lit12 presentation
Literacy	1.1	2.1	3.1	4.1	5.1	6.1	7.1	8.1	9.1	10.1	11.1	12.1
	1.2	2.2	3.2	4.2	5.2	6.2	7.2	8.2	9.2	10.2	11.2	12.2

Numeracy

	Num 1 U&A	Num 2 count	Num 3 number	Num 4 calculate	Num 5 shape	Num 6 measure	Num 7 data
Numeracy	1.1	2.1	3.1	4.1	5.1	6.1	7.1
	1.2	2.2	3.2	4.2	5.2	6.2	7.2

Science

	SC1 Enquiry			SC2 Life processes					SC3 Materials		SC4 Phys processes		
	Sc1.1	Sc1.2	Sc1.3	Sc2.1	Sc2.2	Sc2.3	Sc2.4	Sc2.5	Sc3.1	Sc3.2	Sc4.1	Sc4.2	Sc4.3
Science	1.1a	1.2a	1.3a	2.1a	2.2a	2.3a	2.4a	2.5a	3.1a	3.2a	4.1a	4.2a	4.3a
	1.1b	1.2b	1.3b	2.1b	2.2b	2.3b	2.4b	2.5b	3.1b	3.2b	4.1b	4.2b	4.3b
	1.1c	1.2c	1.3c	2.1c	2.2c	2.3c		2.5c	3.1c		4.1c	4.2c	4.3c
	1.1d				2.2d				3.1d				4.3d
					2.2e								
					2.2f								
					2.2g								

ICT

	ICT 1 finding out		ICT 2 ideas	ICT 3 reviewing	ICT 4 breadth
ICT	1.1a	1.2a	2a	3a	4a
	1.1b	1.2b	2b	3b	4b
	1.1c	1.2c		3c	4c
		1.2d			

D&T

	D&T 1 developing	D&T 2 tool use	D&T 3 evaluating	D&T 4 materials	D&T 5 breadth
D&T	1a	2a	3a	4a	5a
	1b	2b	3b	4b	5b
	1c	2c			5c
	1d	2d			
	1e	2e			

History

	H1 chronology	H2 events, people	H3 interpret	H4 enquire	H5 org & comm	H6 breadth
History	1a	2a	3a	4a	5a	6a
	1b	2b		4b		6b
						6c
						6d

Geography

	G1.1 & G1.2 enquiry		G2 places	G3 processes	G4 environment	G5 breadth
Geography	1.1a	1.2a	2a	3a	4a	5a
	1.1b	1.2b	2b	3b	4b	5b
	1.1c	1.2c	2c			5c
	1.1d	1.2d	2d			5d
			2e			

Music

	M1 performing	M2 composing	M3 appraising	M4 listening	M5 breadth
Music	1a	2a	3a	4a	5a
	1b	2b	3b	4b	5b
	1c			4c	5c
					5d

PHSE & C

	PSHEC1 conf & resp	PSHEC2 citizenship	PSHEC3 health	PSHEC4 relationships
PHSE & C	1a	2a	3a	4a
	1b	2b	3b	4b
	1c	2c	3c	4c
	1d	2d	3d	4d
	1e	2e	3e	4e
		2f	3f	
		2g	3g	
		2h		

Art & Design

	A&D1 ideas	A&D2 making	A&D3 evaluating	A&D4 materials	A&D5 breadth
Art & Design	1a	2a	3a	4a	5a
	1b	2b	3b	4b	5b
		2c		4c	5c
					5d

PE

	PE1 devel skills	PE2 apply skills	PE3 evaluate	PE4 fitness	PE5 breadth
PE	1a	2a	3a	4a	5a dance
	1b	2b	3b	4b	5b games
		2c	3c		5c gym

Critical skills	Thinking Skills
problem solving	observing
decision making	classifying
critical thinking	prediction
creative thinking	making inferences
communication	problem solving
organisation	drawing conclusions
management	
leadership	

Wire

Wire

Previous experience in the Foundation Stage. Some settings are quite adventurous in offering children wire to work with. However, many children will have limited experience of working with wire, although they may have:

* experimented with pipe cleaners;
* worked with an artist or practitioner to make things from chicken wire. They might have helped to add clay, plaster of paris or paper to wire to form a variety of shapes;
* woven ribbon or other material through wire of different sorts;
* used wire to make mobiles and hangings;

N.B. Before allowing the children to work with wire be sure to spend time making sure that they know how to do this safely!

Pause for thought

In the early stages of working with these materials it is crucial to continue to observe the children. Only by doing this can you set developmentally appropriate challenges and provocations. The ideas listed here are offered as suggestions; the most exciting challenges will arise from children's own interests and motivations, which will only become apparent as you spend time with them, watching and joining them in their play. As you do this, you will be moving between the three interconnecting roles of observer, co-player, extender described below, and will be able to decide what you need to do next to take the learning forward.

The responsive adult (see page 5)

In three interconnecting roles, the responsive adult will be:

* observing
* listening
* interpreting

observer

* **modelling**
* **playing alongside**
* **offering suggestions**
* **responding sensitively**
* **initiating with care!**

co-player

* discussing ideas
* sharing thinking
* modelling new skills
* asking open questions
* being an informed extender
* instigating ideas & thoughts
* supporting children as they make links in learning
* making possibilities evident
* introducing new ideas and resources
* offering challenges and provocations

extender

Offering challenges and provocations - some ideas:

Try to make wire available for construction and creative projects. Have clear rules and start with small lengths of plastic covered wire or pipe cleaners. Children need to be shown how to bend and shape the wire, and to cut it with wire snips.

? Can you design some jewellery and then make it by bending, twisting and decorating your wire? Can you make crowns, bracelets and necklaces? Can you add beads and sequins?

? Can you design and make some hanging decorations for the classroom and the outdoor area?

? Find out all you can about Dream Catchers and see if you can make some.

? Can you make some garden sculptures and incorporate twigs, leaves and bark into your designs?

? Google 'wire sculptures'. Use what you find as inspiration for some work of your own.

? Can you bend some wire to make interesting shapes and then cover it with papier mache?

? Google 'Anthony Gormley'. Look at some of the ways he uses wire to make sculptures. See if this gives you ideas for sculptures of your own.

? Can you work as a group or a class to make a large animal, person or mythical creature from wire, coat hangers, wire netting and other sorts of wire? Collect lots of different sorts of wire before you start, and work out of doors if you can. Decorate your wire sculpture with metal objects such as ring pulls from cans, foil, metal cases from food items such as jam tarts, bits of chain, washers, nuts and bolts. Fix the decorations with fuse wire, it's easier to manage.

Ready for more?

- Can you make a sculpture that uses several different types of wire? You could collect fuse wire, plastic coated wire, coat hangers, green garden wire, cable, jeweller's wire, curtain wire, wire netting - there are hundreds of different sorts!
- Can you twist wire to make a variety of three dimensional shapes? Hang these up to make a mathematical mobile.
- Can you 'write' your name in wire? Put 'wire name' in Google Images for some ideas of how to do it.
- Now can you work as a group or a class to 'write' a short verse in wire?
- Can you make a den by wiring twigs and branches together and covering your shelter with plastic sheet or thin fabric?
- Can you use wire to make a house for a toy or a garage for a car? How could you make this waterproof?
- Look a www.nshima.com/2008/05/the-creative-ki.html to find information about some boys in Zimbabwe who make cars from wire.
- Can you use wire to make a boat? Can you make it waterproof and find a way to make it float?
- Can you think of other materials that could be combined with wire to make structures and sculptures, for example, rolled up newspaper or cardboard?

Materials, equipment suppliers, websites, books and other references

The following sorts of wire are suitable for children to use. You may need to provide some adult help with some, but with care and training, children can work competently to produce wire creations.

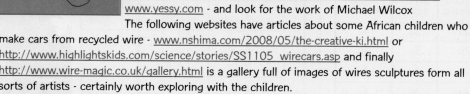

* soldering wire is very soft and can be easily bent by hand;
* picture hanging wire comes in gold and silver;
* jewellery wire can be purchased on line from hundreds of craft sites;
* electrical cable can be stripped of its outer casing to reveal several strands of plastic covered wire;
* wire coat hangers are very useful for making mobiles and hanging creations;
* wire netting is great for making big sculptures;
* plastic bag ties are safe and cheap;
* copper wire is easily formed round simple objects.

Offer children plenty of other objects to add to their creations - beads, feathers, sequins, tape, ribbon pieces, fabric scraps, coloured paper, old pieces of jewellery etc.

Simple tools, such as wire snips, pliers, silversmithing tools all come in small sizes suitable for children to choose. They also help with winding wire round objects to make spirals and other shapes.

Google 'wire sculpture' 'wire structure' 'wire sculpture reggio' 'wire sculpture' 'wire sculpture kids' for children's work.

Some **web sites**:
http://www.whiteoakschool.com/reggio-resources/ for Reggio Emilia resources and magazines
wire artists http://www.vistagallery.com/html/sten_hoiland.html or www.yessy.com - and look for the work of Michael Wilcox
The following websites have articles about some African children who make cars from recycled wire - www.nshima.com/2008/05/the-creative-ki.html or http://www.highlightskids.com/science/stories/SS1105_wirecars.asp and finally http://www.wire-magic.co.uk/gallery.html is a gallery full of images of wires sculptures form all sorts of artists - certainly worth exploring with the children.

Rush on Paper. An Introduction to Modelling Wire and Paper Figures; Peter Rush; James Hockey Gallery

Curriculum coverage grid overleaf

Potential NC KS1 Curriculum Coverage through the provocations suggested for wire.

Full version of KS1 PoS on pages 69-74
Photocopiable version on page 8

Literacy

Literacy	Lit 1 speak	Lit 2 listen	Lit 3 group	Lit 4 drama	Lit 5 word	Lit 6 spell	Lit 7 text1	Lit 8 text2	Lit 9 text3	Lit10 text4	Lit11 sentence	Lit12 presentation
	1.1	2.1	3.1	4.1	5.1	6.1	7.1	8.1	9.1	10.1	11.1	12.1
	1.2	2.2	3.2	4.2	5.2	6.2	7.2	8.2	9.2	10.2	11.2	12.2

Numeracy

Numeracy	Num 1 U&A	Num 2 count	Num 3 number	Num 4 calculate	Num 5 shape	Num 6 measure	Num 7 data
	1.1	2.1	3.1	4.1	5.1	6.1	7.1
	1.2	2.2	3.2	4.2	5.2	6.2	7.2

Science

Science	SC1 Enquiry			SC2 Life processes					SC3 Materials		SC4 Phys processes		
	Sc1.1	Sc1.2	Sc1.3	Sc2.1	Sc2.2	Sc2.3	Sc2.4	Sc2.5	Sc3.1	Sc3.2	Sc4.1	Sc4.2	Sc4.3
	1.1a	1.2a	1.3a	2.1a	2.2a	2.3a	2.4a	2.5a	3.1a	3.2a	4.1a	4.2a	4.3a
	1.1b	1.2b	1.3b	2.1b	2.2b	2.3b	2.4b	2.5b	3.1b	3.2b	4.1b	4.2b	4.3b
	1.1c	1.2c	1.3c	2.1c	2.2c	2.3c		2.5c	3.1c		4.1c	4.2c	4.3c
	1.1d				2.2d				3.1d				4.3d
					2.2e								
					2.2f								
					2.2g								

ICT

ICT	ICT 1 finding out		ICT 2 ideas	ICT 3 reviewing	ICT 4 breadth
	1.1a	1.2a	2a	3a	4a
	1.1b	1.2b	2b	3b	4b
	1.1c	1.2c		3c	4c
		1.2d			

D&T

D&T	D&T 1 developing	D&T 2 tool use	D&T 3 evaluating	D&T 4 materials	D&T 5 breadth
	1a	2a	3a	4a	5a
	1b	2b	3b	4b	5b
	1c	2c			5c
	1d	2d			
	1e	2e			

History

History	H1 chronology	H2 events, people	H3 interpret	H4 enquire	H5 org & comm	H6 breadth
	1a	2a	3a	4a	5a	6a
	1b	2b		4b		6b
						6c
						6d

Geography

Geography	G1.1 & G1.2 enquiry		G2 places	G3 processes	G4 environment	G5 breadth
	1.1a	1.2a	2a	3a	4a	5a
	1.1b	1.2b	2b	3b	4b	5b
	1.1c	1.2c	2c			5c
	1.1d	1.2d	2d			5d
			2e			

Music

Music	M1 performing	M2 composing	M3 appraising	M4 listening	M5 breadth
	1a	2a	3a	4a	5a
	1b	2b	3b	4b	5b
	1c			4c	5c
					5d

PHSE & C

PHSE & C	PSHEC1 conf & resp	PSHEC2 citizenship	PSHEC3 health	PSHEC4 relationships
	1a	2a	3a	4a
	1b	2b	3b	4b
	1c	2c	3c	4c
	1d	2d	3d	4d
	1e	2e	3e	4e
		2f	3f	
		2g	3g	
		2h		

Art & Design

Art & Design	A&D1 ideas	A&D2 making	A&D3 evaluating	A&D4 materials	A&D5 breadth
	1a	2a	3a	4a	5a
	1b	2b	3b	4b	5b
		2c		4c	5c
					5d

PE

PE	PE1 devel skills	PE2 apply skills	PE3 evaluate	PE4 fitness	PE5 breadth
	1a	2a	3a	4a	5a dance
	1b	2b	3b	4b	5b games
		2c	3c		5c gym

Critical skills	Thinking Skills
problem solving	observing
decision making	classifying
critical thinking	prediction
creative thinking	making inferences
communication	problem solving
organisation	drawing conclusions
management	
leadership	

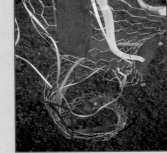

Paper Pulp

Paper Pulp

Previous experience in the Foundation Stage
Paper is a free resource, and many children will have played with shreddings and torn paper. Some will have made papier maché with strips of sheets of paper to make:
* models;
* scenes for small world play;
* bowls and small plates;
* coverings for pots and tubs;
* covering balloons for instruments and puppet heads.

These activities may have evolved around:
* stories and poems;
* puppet play;
* seasonal themes and gift making;
* themes from nature;

and been inspired by art work from a wide range of cultures.

Pause for thought
In the early stages of working with these materials it is crucial to continue to observe the children. Only by doing this can you set developmentally appropriate challenges and provocations. The ideas listed here are offered as suggestions; the most exciting challenges will arise from children's own interests and motivations, which will only become apparent as you spend time with them, watching and joining them in their play. As you do this, you will be moving between the three interconnecting roles of observer, co-player, extender described below, and will be able to decide what you need to do next to take the learning forward.

The responsive adult (see page 5)

In three interconnecting roles, the responsive adult will be:

observer

* observing
* listening
* interpreting

co-player

* **modelling**
* **playing alongside**
* **offering suggestions**
* **responding sensitively**
* **initiating with care!**

extender

* discussing ideas
* sharing thinking
* modelling new skills
* asking open questions
* being an informed extender
* instigating ideas and thoughts
* supporting children as they make links in learning
* making possibilities evident
* introducing new ideas and resources
* offering challenges and provocations

Offering challenges and provocations - some ideas:

Recycled paper is a free resource which is ideal for this activity. Shreddings from a shredder, scrap paper, newspaper or junk mail can also be used. Avoid very shiny paper from magazines, and be aware that the print will affect the colour of the pulp, and may colour children's hands!

? Collect some scrap paper and tear it into very small pieces. Add some cellulose paste and water to make a sloshy mixture. Stir it with a stick or your hand, squeezing the paper so it dissolves in the liquid. Keep <u>stirring for a day</u> until the pulp is well mixed and the paper is soaked right through, but not too wet. If it is too runny, add some more paper.

? The next day, tip some of the paper pulp on to a board or table top, and squeeze it with your hands. Keep squishing till the paper pulp is smooth. Now use your hands to mould the pulp into a shape. Watch and feel how it behaves in your hands. Can you build tall structures?

? Use some of your pulp to make a bowl or cup. You may need to squeeze some of the water out with your hands before you start. When you have made your cup or bowl, leave it somewhere warm to dry. It may take several days to dry right through - putting it near a radiator or in a VERY low oven will speed up the process. Microwaving <u>doesn't</u> work.

? Use something as a shaper or former for your paper pulp - you could use small bowls, yogurt pots, plant pots or anything with a smooth surface. Turn the shaper upside down and put pulp all over it. Smooth the pulp with your hands, or leave it rough, whichever you wish. When the pulp is dry, you should be able to remove the shaper. What does the inside of your creation feel like? Is it the same as the outside?

? Try some different shapers and decorate them with paint, felt pens, beads, sequins and other small objects.

Ready for more?

- Do an experiment. Make pulp with different sorts of paper. Try:
  * shiny magazine paper;
  * crepe or tissue paper;
  * paper towels;
  * tissues or kitchen roll;
  * newspaper.

  Which works best - which is the least successful?

- Work as a class. Collect newspapers from everyone you know, and make a huge amount of pulp in buckets. Now get a big sheet of wood or strong card and use your paper pulp to make a landscape. You could make:
  * a moon or space scene;
  * a historic scene;
  * high mountains;
  * a fantasy landscape.
  * a model of your school or your area.

  Dont forget to take photos!

  Remember that paper pulp takes a long time to dry, so be patient! When it is dry you could paint the landscape. What could you use for trees? For roads or streets? For buildings? For castles and caves? For rivers and lakes? Can you find or make some people the right scale or size for your landscape?

- Find some wire netting and see if you can make a big sculpture using wire netting and lots of paper pulp.

Materials, equipment suppliers, websites, books and other references

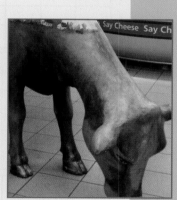

Any sort of paper can be used for sculptures and creations. newspaper and other 'pulpy' papers are best for making papier mache or paper pulp - avoid shiny magazine paper - it doesn't soak up the paste well. Collect paper that can be recycled into pulp, and add some texture and colouring such as:

* crepe paper to colour pulp;
* sand, sawdust or compost to add texture;
* seeds of all sorts such as grass seed, melon or sunflower seeds;
* herbs and spices for texture and perfume;
* aromatherapy oils;
* paint or food colouring;
* glitter or sequins.

For images of paper sculpture and other work, try **Google Images**, 'paper sculpture' 'paper weaving' 'papier mache sculpture' 'paper craft'.

Some suitable **books to use with younger children** include:

Papier-mache for Kids; Sheila McGraw; Firefly Books
Art Attack: How to Papier Mache;Karen Brown; Panini
Papier Mache; Ray Gibson; Usborne
Creating with Papier Mache; Victoria Seix; Blackbirch Press
Papier Mache; Design Eye Publishing
Papier Mache; Judy Balchin; Search Press

Decorative Painting; Judy Balchin; Search Press
Spectacular Paper Sculptures; Ron Van Der Meer; Robin Corey Books
Complete Book of Paper Mask Making; Michael Grater; Dover Pubs
Paper, Scissors, Sculpt!: Creating Cut-and-fold Animals; Ben A. Gonzales; Sterling Juvenile
Mobiles and Other Paper Wind Catchers; Phyllis Fiarotta; Sterling
Look What You Can Make with Tubes; Margie Hayes Richmond; Boyds Mills Press
Look What You Can Make from Paper Plates; Margie Hayes Richmond; Boyds Mills Press
Look What You Can Make with Newspapers, Magazines, and Greeting Cards; Kathy Ross; Boyds Mills Press
Look What You Can Make with Plastic Bottles and Tubs; Kathy Ross; Boyds Mills Press

Curriculum coverage grid overleaf

Potential NC KS1 Curriculum Coverage through the provocations suggested for paper pulp.

Full version of KS1 PoS on pages 69-74
Photocopiable version on page 8

Literacy

Lit 1 speak	Lit 2 listen	Lit 3 group	Lit 4 drama	Lit 5 word	Lit 6 spell	Lit 7 text1	Lit 8 text2	Lit 9 text3	Lit10 text4	Lit11 sentence	Lit12 presentation
1.1	2.1	3.1	4.1	5.1	6.1	7.1	8.1	9.1	10.1	11.1	12.1
1.2	2.2	3.2	4.2	5.2	6.2	7.2	8.2	9.2	10.2	11.2	12.2

Numeracy

Num 1 U&A	Num 2 count	Num 3 number	Num 4 calculate	Num 5 shape	Num 6 measure	Num 7 data
1.1	2.1	3.1	4.1	5.1	6.1	7.1
1.2	2.2	3.2	4.2	5.2	6.2	7.2

Science

SC1 Enquiry			SC2 Life processes					SC3 Materials		SC4 Phys processes		
Sc1.1	Sc1.2	Sc1.3	Sc2.1	Sc2.2	Sc2.3	Sc2.4	Sc2.5	Sc3.1	Sc3.2	Sc4.1	Sc4.2	Sc4.3
1.1a	1.2a	1.3a	2.1a	2.2a	2.3a	2.4a	2.5a	3.1a	3.2a	4.1a	4.2a	4.3a
1.1b	1.2b	1.3b	2.1b	2.2b	2.3b	2.4b	2.5b	3.1b	3.2b	4.1b	4.2b	4.3b
1.1c	1.2c	1.3c	2.1c	2.2c	2.3c		2.5c	3.1c		4.1c	4.2c	4.3c
1.1d				2.2d				3.1d				4.3d
				2.2e								
				2.2f								
				2.2g								

ICT

ICT 1 finding out		ICT 2 ideas	ICT 3 reviewing	ICT 4 breadth
1.1a	1.2a	2a	3a	4a
1.1b	1.2b	2b	3b	4b
1.1c	1.2c		3c	4c
	1.2d			

D&T

D&T 1 developing	D&T 2 tool use	D&T 3 evaluating	D&T 4 materials	D&T 5 breadth
1a	2a	3a	4a	5a
1b	2b	3b	4b	5b
1c	2c			5c
1d	2d			
1e	2e			

History

H1 chronology	H2 events, people	H3 interpret	H4 enquire	H5 org & comm	H6 breadth
1a	2a	3a	4a	5a	6a
1b	2b		4b		6b
					6c
					6d

Geography

G1.1 & G1.2 enquiry		G2 places	G3 processes	G4 environment	G5 breadth
1.1a	1.2a	2a	3a	4a	5a
1.1b	1.2b	2b	3b	4b	5b
1.1c	1.2c	2c			5c
1.1d	1.2d	2d			5d
		2e			

Music

M1 performing	M2 composing	M3 appraising	M4 listening	M5 breadth
1a	2a	3a	4a	5a
1b	2b	3b	4b	5b
1c			4c	5c
				5d

PHSE & C

PSHEC1 conf & resp	PSHEC2 citizenship	PSHEC3 health	PSHEC4 relationships
1a	2a	3a	4a
1b	2b	3b	4b
1c	2c	3c	4c
1d	2d	3d	4d
1e	2e	3e	4e
	2f	3f	
	2g	3g	
	2h		

Art & Design

A&D1 ideas	A&D2 making	A&D3 evaluating	A&D4 materials	A&D5 breadth
1a	2a	3a	4a	5a
1b	2b	3b	4b	5b
	2c		4c	5c
				5d

PE

PE1 devel skills	PE2 apply skills	PE3 evaluate	PE4 fitness	PE5 breadth
1a	2a	3a	4a	5a dance
1b	2b	3b	4b	5b games
	2c	3c		5c gym

Critical skills	Thinking Skills
problem solving	observing
decision making	classifying
critical thinking	prediction
creative thinking	making inferences
communication	problem solving
organisation	drawing conclusions
management	
leadership	

Ice

Ice

Previous experience in the Foundation Stage
Exploring and experimenting with ice is a common activity in early year's settings so most children will have some experience of the properties of ice in one form or another. They may have:
* played with ice as part of water play;
* eaten ice lollies;
* observed icicles and frozen puddles in the winter;
* carried out experiments with ice;
* made ice shapes in the freezer in containers of different sorts and sizes.

Pause for thought
In the early stages of working with these materials it is crucial to continue to observe the children. Only by doing this can you set developmentally appropriate challenges and provocations. The ideas listed here are offered as suggestions; the most exciting challenges will arise from children's own interests and motivations, which will only become apparent as you spend time with them, watching and joining them in their play. As you do this, you will be moving between the three interconnecting roles of observer, co-player, extender described below, and will be able to decide what you need to do next to take the learning forward.

The responsive adult (see page 5)
In three interconnecting roles, the responsive adult will be:

observer
* observing
* listening
* interpreting

co-player
* **modelling**
* **playing alongside**
* **offering suggestions**
* **responding sensitively**
* **initiating with care!**

extender
* discussing ideas
* sharing thinking
* modelling new skills
* asking open questions
* being an informed extender
* instigating ideas and thoughts
* supporting children as they make links in learning
* making possibilities evident
* introducing new ideas and resources
* offering challenges and provocations

Offering challenges and provocations - some ideas:

? Make a collection of interesting cartons and containers that could be used to freeze water in. You should be able to find lots of recycled containers, but think of some more unusual ones too. You can try anything that doesn't leak!

? Can you make some moulds of your own with plasticine and freeze water in these?

? Can you design some fruit slushes for your friends to try? How many different flavours can you create?

? Can you design a range of ice lollies using different flavours of fruit juice?
  • How many different shapes can you make?
  • How many different flavours?
  • How many different colours?

? Can you think of ways to make a multi-coloured ice lolly? How did you do it?

? What is the largest block of ice you can create? Try all sorts of containers.

? Can you create an ice-sculpture by chipping bits from a large block of ice? NB. Remember to wear goggles to protect your eyes!

? Try freezing objects into blocks if ice, for example a key. How long do you think it will take to get the key out?

? Can you write a story about the frozen key, how it got frozen and what happened to it next?

? Get a lot of ice cubes (you can buy a bag from a supermarket) and see if you can make the cubes into a sculpture.

Ready for more?

- Try freezing flowers into ice cubes. Make arrangements with your frozen ice cubes and photograph them to make cards, pictures, book marks and other designs.
- Experiment with plastic bags and string. Put some water into the bag. Tie it off with string and then add more water to make some interesting shapes.
- Use frozen blocks and ice cubes to make a structure for some small world arctic characters. Can you built a frozen environment for small world polar bears, penguins and other arctic creatures?
- Hold some competitions with your friends to see who can get a block of ice to melt the fastest. Try different ways and graph the results.
- Hold some competitions to see who can keep a block of ice frozen for the longest period of time. What are the best insulators?
- Freeze string into ice cubes so that you can use them to make mobiles and decorations.
- In winter, go on an ice hunt and make the ice into mobiles and other decorations.
- Google 'ice sculptures' and 'ice hotel'. See if you can find new ideas for ice sculptures.
- Make some ice balloons by filling balloons with water. Freeze interesting things inside like glitter or tinsel.

Materials, equipment suppliers, websites, books and other references

Some ideas for **resources and equipment**:

Making ice is a cheap and interesting activity if you have a freezer at school or are prepared to use your own at home. Encourage the children to be adventurous in the moulds they use and the way they use the ice for constructions. Try some of these:

* recycled containers such as yogurt pots, plastic bottles;
* the liners from chocolates, sweet boxes, or food trays;
* unusual items such as plastic or rubber gloves;
* balloons with or without small objects inside;
* big containers such as ice cream tubs.

If you don't have easy access to a freezer, you can do a lot of interesting activities with bags of ice cubes form a freezer centre or a supermarket. Some children may like to work with gloves. Collect interesting items to freeze in the ice - these can include:

* small toys;
* beads, sequins, seeds;
* leaves, flowers, petals, grass;

Google Images 'ice festival' for pictures of coloured ice sculptures and whole buildings or 'ice cube flower'. Or try some of these websites:

http://www.grandeurice.com/ and click on 'gallery' for ice sculptures

http://www.bbc.co.uk/norfolk/content/image_galleries/events_ice_sculpture_20071216_gallery.shtml for images of an ice sculpture trail

www.icesculpture.co.uk/ for more images, and for instructions for a glowing ice ball - http://portlandoregonweddingphotographer.wordpress.com/2008/05/19/how-to-make-a-glowing-ice-ball/ a video.

Books and Publications:

Midsummer Snowballs; Andy Goldsworthy; Thames & Hudson is a book about the huge snowballs that the artist placed around London one summer. He had frozen snow during the winter and then left them out in June! See the report on http://news.bbc.co.uk/1/hi/uk/800916.stm or put 'goldsworthy snowballs' in Google Images to see the snowballs and some other ice sculptures he has made.

Curriculum coverage grid overleaf

Potential NC KS1 Curriculum Coverage through the provocations suggested for ice.

Full version of KS1 PoS on pages 69-74
Photocopiable version on page 8

Literacy	Lit 1 speak	Lit 2 listen	Lit 3 group	Lit 4 drama	Lit 5 word	Lit 6 spell	Lit 7 text1	Lit 8 text2	Lit 9 text3	Lit10 text4	Lit11 sen-tence	Lit12 present ation
	1.1	2.1	3.1	4.1	5.1	6.1	7.1	8.1	9.1	10.1	11.1	12.1
	1.2	2.2	3.2	4.2	5.2	6.2	7.2	8.2	9.2	10.2	11.2	12.2

Numeracy	Num 1 U&A	Num 2 count	Num 3 number	Num 4 calculate	Num 5 shape	Num 6 measure	Num 7 data
	1.1	2.1	3.1	4.1	5.1	6.1	7.1
	1.2	2.2	3.2	4.2	5.2	6.2	7.2

Science	SC1 Enquiry			SC2 Life processes					SC3 Materials		SC4 Phys processes		
	Sc1.1	Sc1.2	Sc1.3	Sc2.1	Sc2.2	Sc2.3	Sc2.4	Sc2.5	Sc3.1	Sc3.2	Sc4.1	Sc4.2	Sc4.3
	1.1a	1.2a	1.3a	2.1a	2.2a	2.3a	2.4a	2.5a	3.1a	3.2a	4.1a	4.2a	4.3a
	1.1b	1.2b	1.3b	2.1b	2.2b	2.3b	2.4b	2.5b	3.1b	3.2b	4.1b	4.2b	4.3b
	1.1c	1.2c	1.3c	2.1c	2.2c	2.3c		2.5c	3.1c		4.1c	4.2c	4.3c
	1.1d				2.2d				3.1d				4.3d
					2.2e								
					2.2f								
					2.2g								

ICT	ICT 1 finding out		ICT 2 ideas	ICT 3 reviewing	ICT 4 breadth
	1.1a	1.2a	2a	3a	4a
	1.1b	1.2b	2b	3b	4b
	1.1c	1.2c		3c	4c
		1.2d			

D&T	D&T 1 developing	D&T 2 tool use	D&T 3 evaluating	D&T 4 materials	D&T 5 breadth
	1a	2a	3a	4a	5a
	1b	2b	3b	4b	5b
	1c	2c			5c
	1d	2d			
	1e	2e			

History	H1 chron-ology	H2 events, people	H3 inter-pret	H4 enquire	H5 org & comm	H6 breadth
	1a	2a	3a	4a	5a	6a
	1b	2b		4b		6b
						6c
						6d

Geog-raphy	G1.1 & G1.2 enquiry		G2 places	G3 processes	G4 environment	G5 breadth
	1.1a	1.2a	2a	3a	4a	5a
	1.1b	1.2b	2b	3b	4b	5b
	1.1c	1.2c	2c			5c
	1.1d	1.2d	2d			5d
			2e			

Music	M1 performing	M2 composing	M3 appraising	M4 listening	M5 breadth
	1a	2a	3a	4a	5a
	1b	2b	3b	4b	5b
	1c			4c	5c
					5d

PHSE & C	PSHEC1 conf & resp	PSHEC2 citizenship	PSHEC3 health	PSHEC4 relationships
	1a	2a	3a	4a
	1b	2b	3b	4b
	1c	2c	3c	4c
	1d	2d	3d	4d
	1e	2e	3e	4e
		2f	3f	
		2g	3g	
		2h		

Art& Design	A&D1 ideas	A&D2 making	A&D3 evaluating	A&D4 materials	A&D5 breadth
	1a	2a	3a	4a	5a
	1b	2b	3b	4b	5b
		2c		4c	5c
					5d

PE	PE1 devel skills	PE2 apply skills	PE3 evaluate	PE4 fitness	PE5 breadth
	1a	2a	3a	4a	5a dance
	1b	2b	3b	4b	5b games
		2c	3c		5c gym

Critical skills	Thinking Skills
problem solving	observing
decision making	classifying
critical thinking	prediction
creative thinking	making inferences
communication	problem solving
organisation	drawing conclusions
management	
leadership	

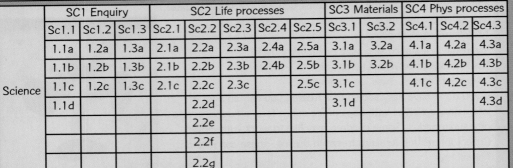

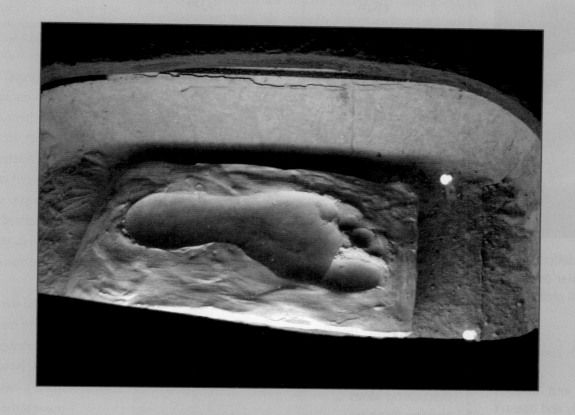

Plaster and Plaster Bandages

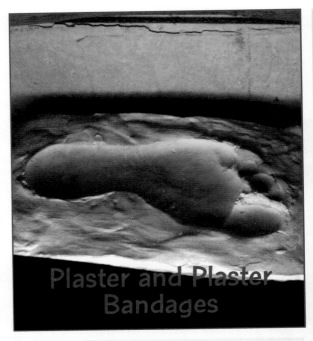

Plaster and Plaster Bandages

Previous experience in the Foundation Stage

Children may never have used plaster or plaster bandages before. If they have, it will probably be in supervised activities such as:

* making hand or foot prints;
* wrapping simple objects with plaster bandage.

Plaster of Paris is a complex and difficult material to use. It dries very quickly and doesn't re-constitute if you add water. It is also fairly expensive for free use.

However it does have unique properties which older children can fruitfully explore, making and discussing scientific observations, learning about the properties of materials and investigating change.

Pause for thought

In the early stages of working with these materials it is crucial to continue to observe the children. Only by doing this can you set developmentally appropriate challenges and provocations. The ideas listed here are offered as suggestions; the most exciting challenges will arise from children's own interests and motivations, which will only become apparent as you spend time with them, watching and joining them in their play. As you do this, you will be moving between the three interconnecting roles of observer, co-player, extender described below, and will be able to decide what you need to do next to take the learning forward.

The responsive adult (see page 5)

In three interconnecting roles, the responsive adult will be:

* observing
* listening
* interpreting

observer

* **modelling**
* **playing alongside**
* **offering suggestions**
* **responding sensitively**
* **initiating with care!**

co-player

* discussing ideas
* sharing thinking
* modelling new skills
* asking open questions
* being an informed extender
* instigating ideas and thoughts
* supporting children as they make links in learning
* making possibilities evident
* introducing new ideas and resources
* offering challenges and provocations

extender

Offering challenges and provocations - some ideas:

Plaster of Paris is a useful substance for exploring how materials change and those which cannot be returned to their original form. Plaster needs careful supervision because the methods are crucial. However, plaster bandage is a fascinating resource which children will love to use in constructing sculptures and objects.

? Work in a group to explore some Plaster of Paris. Find some small containers, put some small objects in the bottom of them and pour a mixture of plaster and water into the pots. Hold the pots. Can you feel anything? Watch the plaster - what is happening? When the plaster is dry tip it out of the pot and see what has happened to the objects you put in the bottom?

? Use this method to make some bird cakes with plaster and bird seed. How can you do it? Do the birds like their cakes? Take some photos of which birds come to your food.

? Now can you think of some other ways to use the plaster of Paris to make casts and patterns?

? Find some plaster bandage (called Modroc) and read the instructions. How could you use the plaster bandage to:
  * make a cast of your hand or foot;
  * make structures by putting it over things?

? Look outside for some footprints or other marks in the mud or soil. Can you use plaster of Paris to make casts of these prints? Remember that plaster sets very quickly, so you will have to work fast!

? Find some sticks and twigs. Set the twigs in small pots of plaster and decorate them. You could use beads, sequins, glitter, ribbon, or 'found objects' such as leaves, shells, bark or moss.

Ready for more?

- Make a bigger version of the twig sculpture using a larger branch and working as a group. You could spray or paint the branch and decorate it for a festival. If you dip Modroc bandages in water and lay them flat to dry, you can cut them into lacy decorations which you can spray and hang on your branch.

- Find out about the Invisible Man, and why he had to wrap his head in bandages. Can you make an invisible man model using a small world figure? Make up a story about him, and take some photos for a display, a book or a Power Point presentation.

- Find out about Anthony Gormley who makes sculptures from his own body by wrapping it in bandages. Can you use a small world toy or superhero model to make a sculpture with plaster bandages?

- Collect some recycled materials and use these with plaster bandages to make some abstract sculptures. Look on http://artseducation.suite101.com/article.cfm/plaster_bandage_s culptures for help in doing this. You could work together to make something big for your playground or garden. If you want to make an outdoor sculpture, use outdoor paint to protect it from the weather.

- Can you think of a way to make a mask from plaster bandage?

Materials, equipment suppliers, websites, books and other references

Get Modroc Bandage from:

www.craftmill.co.uk - modroc bandages and sheets, air drying clay, tools, shaped cutters

http://www.modroc.com/modroctips.htm - great tips for using modroc

http://www.accessart.org.uk/modroc.php - how to use modroc

www.tts-group.co.uk - for modroc and plaster of paris, newclay, tools, rollers, rolling pins, buff and red clay.

You can get casting plaster from chemists and from specialist craft shops and websites.

Find out how to makeplaster casts on these sites:

www.wildyorkshire.co.uk/naturediary/docs/2003/5/5.html footprints in the mud, and

www.rspb.org.uk/youth/makeanddo/activities/tracks.asp for a download of a simple guide to the footprints of common birds and animals.

Google Images

'footprints plaster' 'plaster casting' 'plaster cast head' 'plaster cast hand' 'plaster foot'

For guidance on making landscapes, look at sites for model railway enthusiasts or architects.

http://fun.familyeducation.com/childrens-art-activities/sculpting/40287.html has an activity called plaster box etching.

Books:

Let's Model with Plaster, Eileen Geipel; Evans Bros

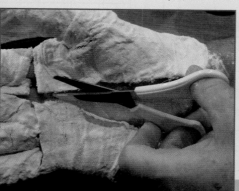

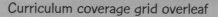

Curriculum coverage grid overleaf

Potential NC KS1 Curriculum Coverage through the provocations suggested for plaster & plaster bandages.

Full version of KS1 PoS on pages 69-74
Photocopiable version on page 8

Literacy

	Lit 1 speak	Lit 2 listen	Lit 3 group	Lit 4 drama	Lit 5 word	Lit 6 spell	Lit 7 text1	Lit 8 text2	Lit 9 text3	Lit10 text4	Lit11 sentence	Lit12 presentation
	1.1	2.1	3.1	4.1	5.1	6.1	7.1	8.1	9.1	10.1	11.1	12.1
	1.2	2.2	3.2	4.2	5.2	6.2	7.2	8.2	9.2	10.2	11.2	12.2

Numeracy

	Num 1 U&A	Num 2 count	Num 3 number	Num 4 calculate	Num 5 shape	Num 6 measure	Num 7 data
	1.1	2.1	3.1	4.1	5.1	6.1	7.1
	1.2	2.2	3.2	4.2	5.2	6.2	7.2

Science

	SC1 Enquiry			SC2 Life processes					SC3 Materials		SC4 Phys processes		
	Sc1.1	Sc1.2	Sc1.3	Sc2.1	Sc2.2	Sc2.3	Sc2.4	Sc2.5	Sc3.1	Sc3.2	Sc4.1	Sc4.2	Sc4.3
	1.1a	1.2a	1.3a	2.1a	2.2a	2.3a	2.4a	2.5a	3.1a	3.2a	4.1a	4.2a	4.3a
	1.1b	1.2b	1.3b	2.1b	2.2b	2.3b	2.4b	2.5b	3.1b	3.2b	4.1b	4.2b	4.3b
	1.1c	1.2c	1.3c	2.1c	2.2c	2.3c		2.5c	3.1c		4.1c	4.2c	4.3c
	1.1d				2.2d				3.1d				4.3d
					2.2e								
					2.2f								
					2.2g								

ICT

	ICT 1 finding out		ICT 2 ideas	ICT 3 reviewing	ICT 4 breadth
	1.1a	1.2a	2a	3a	4a
	1.1b	1.2b	2b	3b	4b
	1.1c	1.2c		3c	4c
		1.2d			

D&T

	D&T 1 developing	D&T 2 tool use	D&T 3 evaluating	D&T 4 materials	D&T 5 breadth
	1a	2a	3a	4a	5a
	1b	2b	3b	4b	5b
	1c	2c			5c
	1d	2d			
	1e	2e			

History

	H1 chronology	H2 events, people	H3 interpret	H4 enquire	H5 org & comm	H6 breadth
	1a	2a	3a	4a	5a	6a
	1b	2b		4b		6b
						6c
						6d

Geography

	G1.1 & G1.2 enquiry		G2 places	G3 processes	G4 environment	G5 breadth
	1.1a	1.2a	2a	3a	4a	5a
	1.1b	1.2b	2b	3b	4b	5b
	1.1c	1.2c	2c			5c
	1.1d	1.2d	2d			5d
			2e			

Music

	M1 performing	M2 composing	M3 appraising	M4 listening	M5 breadth
	1a	2a	3a	4a	5a
	1b	2b	3b	4b	5b
	1c			4c	5c
					5d

PHSE & C

	PSHEC1 conf & resp	PSHEC2 citizenship	PSHEC3 health	PSHEC4 relationships
	1a	2a	3a	4a
	1b	2b	3b	4b
	1c	2c	3c	4c
	1d	2d	3d	4d
	1e	2e	3e	4e
		2f	3f	
		2g	3g	
		2h		

Art & Design

	A&D1 ideas	A&D2 making	A&D3 evaluating	A&D4 materials	A&D5 breadth
	1a	2a	3a	4a	5a
	1b	2b	3b	4b	5b
		2c		4c	5c
					5d

PE

	PE1 devel skills	PE2 apply skills	PE3 evaluate	PE4 fitness	PE5 breadth
	1a	2a	3a	4a	5a dance
	1b	2b	3b	4b	5b games
		2c	3c		5c gym

Critical skills	Thinking Skills
problem solving	observing
decision making	classifying
critical thinking	prediction
creative thinking	making inferences
communication	problem solving
organisation	drawing conclusions
management	
leadership	

Balsa Wood and Sandpaper

Balsa Wood and Sandpaper

Previous experience in the Foundation Stage
Balsa wood is sometimes used in the EYFS for simple woodwork projects as it is soft and easily worked. Children may have:
* seen and worked with balsa wood;
* used sandpaper as part of woodworking play;
* seen balsa wood in models and constructions.

However, these materials - both sandpaper and balsa wood will be new and unfamiliar, needing time for free exploration before introducing provocations and challenges.

Pause for thought
In the early stages of working with these materials it is crucial to continue to observe the children. Only by doing this can you set developmentally appropriate challenges and provocations. The ideas listed here are offered as suggestions; the most exciting challenges will arise from children's own interests and motivations, which will only become apparent as you spend time with them, watching and joining them in their play. As you do this, you will be moving between the three interconnecting roles of observer, co-player, extender described below, and will be able to decide what you need to do next to take the learning forward.

The responsive adult (see page 5)

In three interconnecting roles, the responsive adult will be:

* observing
* listening
* interpreting

observer

* **modelling**
* **playing alongside**
* **offering suggestions**
* **responding sensitively**
* **initiating with care!**

co-player

* discussing ideas
* sharing thinking
* modelling new skills
* asking open questions
* being an informed extender
* instigating ideas and thoughts
* supporting children as they make links in learning
* making possibilities evident
* introducing new ideas and resources
* offering challenges and provocations

extender

Offering challenges and provocations - some ideas:

NOTE: If balsa is an entirely new material for many children, it is really important that they have time to explore and experiment to find out about its properties. Start with some quite thick pieces of wood and some sandpaper or sanding blocks and spend some time discussing what happens and the children's observations on the activity. You may wish to focus on:

* how the wood feels;
* how they think it might be different to other types of wood;
* what they think it is used for;
* the children's own ideas for how they think they could use it.

It may also be useful so show the children how thin balsa wood can be cut with scissors and glued with PVA glue.

? Can you make a boat from a piece of balsa wood, using just sandpaper to shape it? Will it float? Can you make it sink? How did you do this?

? Can your balsa wood boat carry anything - for example, a play person or a small world animal?

? Can you make some jewellery from balsa wood, for example, a pendant, a badge or a brooch? How could you colour the wood?

? Can you find ways of making a hole in a piece of balsa wood?

? Can you make a wood block to use for printing?

? Can you make some furniture for a doll's house by sticking and sanding balsa wood?

? Can you make a castle for some kings, queens and knights?

? Can you create a balsa wood design that you can take rubbings from?

? Can you make your name from balsa wood?

Ready for more?

- Can you make a mythical beast or fantasy figure from balsa wood? You could make the figure flat, so it could play a part in a shadow play or an OHP projection.
- Balsa wood is good for making scenery and environments for plays and stories. Can you make some scenery for the fantasy figure to inhabit? Put 'balsa wood model' in Google Images to see some buildings and other models.
- Can you add other materials to make the habitat for your creature more interesting and exciting?
- Can you build a 'set' for a story, for example, Little Red Riding Hood or Goldilocks and the Three Bears?
- Can you build a balsa wood tower?
- Can you make a balsa wood plane or glider? Will it fly? Look on Google Images 'balsa wood plane' for some ideas.
- Can you make a wild and wonderful bird from balsa wood? Find some feathers to decorate your bird. You could hang it up or even see if it will fly.
- Can you write an information book on the uses of balsa wood?
- Can you write instructions for how to make a balsa wood model such as a plane or a bird? You could take photos as you make one or even get your friend to make a video of you doing it.

Materials, equipment suppliers, websites, books and other references

It's better to get balsa wood from educational or craft suppliers such as www.tts-group.co.uk - who supply balsa wood in packs Try DIY superstores and bargain shops for sandpaper in bulk. Get several different grades for finer or rougher finishes. Use wooden bricks or small wooden offcuts to make sanding blocks, or buy sponge sanding blocks from DIY shops.

Children's tools can be ordered from TTS Group and other school suppliers. Offer children small saws, and good quality scissors for thinner sheets. PVA or wood glue is suitable for construction, and you can stick thin sheets of pieces together to make thicker or bigger parts.

Try looking in *Yellow Pages* for local model making clubs and model makers, who might be willing to give a demonstration.

Investigate Forest Schools and see if you can get involved. There should be a local person to give you advice (try your LA) or look on the Forest Schools site - http://www.forestschools.com/

Try Google and Google Images: 'balsa plane' 'balsa model' 'wooden plane'.

Some books about wood and carving:

Models; Keith Newell; Children's Press
Leroy's Zoo: Featuring the Folk Art Carvings of Leroy Ramon Archuleta; Warren Lowe; Black Belt Press
Daniel's Duck; Clyde Robert Bulla; HarperTrophy
Dream Carver; Diana Cohn; Chronicle Books
The Christmas Miracle of Jonathan Toomey; Susan Wojciechowski; Candlewick Press (the story of a woodcarver and a boy)
The Giant King; Kathleen Pelley; Child & Family Press - a Scottish story of a woodcarver
Wood; Andy Goldsworthy; Harry N. Abrams

Curriculum coverage grid overleaf

Full version of KS1 PoS on pages 69-74
Photocopiable version on page 8

Literacy

Lit 1 speak	Lit 2 listen	Lit 3 group	Lit 4 drama	Lit 5 word	Lit 6 spell	Lit 7 text1	Lit 8 text2	Lit 9 text3	Lit10 text4	Lit11 sentence	Lit12 presentation
1.1	2.1	3.1	4.1	5.1	6.1	7.1	8.1	9.1	10.1	11.1	12.1
1.2	2.2	3.2	4.2	5.2	6.2	7.2	8.2	9.2	10.2	11.2	12.2

Numeracy

Num 1 U&A	Num 2 count	Num 3 number	Num 4 calculate	Num 5 shape	Num 6 measure	Num 7 data
1.1	2.1	3.1	4.1	5.1	6.1	7.1
1.2	2.2	3.2	4.2	5.2	6.2	7.2

Science

SC1 Enquiry			SC2 Life processes					SC3 Materials		SC4 Phys processes		
Sc1.1	Sc1.2	Sc1.3	Sc2.1	Sc2.2	Sc2.3	Sc2.4	Sc2.5	Sc3.1	Sc3.2	Sc4.1	Sc4.2	Sc4.3
1.1a	1.2a	1.3a	2.1a	2.2a	2.3a	2.4a	2.5a	3.1a	3.2a	4.1a	4.2a	4.3a
1.1b	1.2b	1.3b	2.1b	2.2b	2.3b	2.4b	2.5b	3.1b	3.2b	4.1b	4.2b	4.3b
1.1c	1.2c	1.3c	2.1c	2.2c	2.3c		2.5c	3.1c		4.1c	4.2c	4.3c
1.1d				2.2d				3.1d				4.3d
				2.2e								
				2.2f								
				2.2g								

ICT

ICT 1 finding out		ICT 2 ideas	ICT 3 reviewing	ICT 4 breadth
1.1a	1.2a	2a	3a	4a
1.1b	1.2b	2b	3b	4b
1.1c	1.2c		3c	4c
	1.2d			

D&T

D&T 1 developing	D&T 2 tool use	D&T 3 evaluating	D&T 4 materials	D&T 5 breadth
1a	2a	3a	4a	5a
1b	2b	3b	4b	5b
1c	2c			5c
1d	2d			
1e	2e			

History

H1 chronology	H2 events, people	H3 interpret	H4 enquire	H5 org & comm	H6 breadth
1a	2a	3a	4a	5a	6a
1b	2b		4b		6b
					6c
					6d

Geography

G1.1 & G1.2 enquiry		G2 places	G3 processes	G4 environment	G5 breadth
1.1a	1.2a	2a	3a	4a	5a
1.1b	1.2b	2b	3b	4b	5b
1.1c	1.2c	2c			5c
1.1d	1.2d	2d			5d
		2e			

Music

M1 performing	M2 composing	M3 appraising	M4 listening	M5 breadth
1a	2a	3a	4a	5a
1b	2b	3b	4b	5b
1c			4c	5c
				5d

PHSE & C

PSHEC1 conf & resp	PSHEC2 citizenship	PSHEC3 health	PSHEC4 relationships
1a	2a	3a	4a
1b	2b	3b	4b
1c	2c	3c	4c
1d	2d	3d	4d
1e	2e	3e	4e
	2f	3f	
	2g	3g	
	2h		

Art & Design

A&D1 ideas	A&D2 making	A&D3 evaluating	A&D4 materials	A&D5 breadth
1a	2a	3a	4a	5a
1b	2b	3b	4b	5b
	2c		4c	5c
				5d

PE

PE1 devel skills	PE2 apply skills	PE3 evaluate	PE4 fitness	PE5 breadth
1a	2a	3a	4a	5a dance
1b	2b	3b	4b	5b games
	2c	3c		5c gym

Critical skills	Thinking Skills
problem solving	observing
decision making	classifying
critical thinking	prediction
creative thinking	making inferences
communication	problem solving
organisation	drawing conclusions
management	
leadership	

Wax and Soap Carving

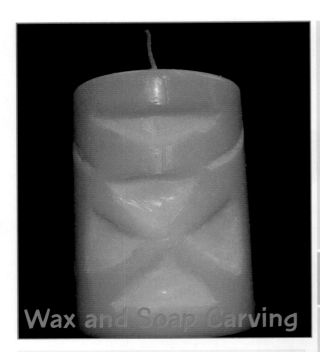

Wax and Soap Carving

Previous experience in the Foundation Stage

These materials may be new to children in Key Stage 1, although soap sculpture may have been offered in the Foundation Stage. Children's experiences of candles and soap may have been limited to:

* night lights and other candles in celebrations and birthdays;
* perfumed candles for special occasions or in Circle Times
* writing with candles and paint in wax resist;
* using wax crayons;
* playing with bars of soap to make bubbles, in play and as part of an activity.

Pause for thought

In the early stages of working with these materials it is crucial to continue to observe the children. Only by doing this can you set developmentally appropriate challenges and provocations. The ideas listed here are offered as suggestions; the most exciting challenges will arise from children's own interests and motivations, which will only become apparent as you spend time with them, watching and joining them in their play. As you do this, you will be moving between the three interconnecting roles of observer, co-player, extender described below, and will be able to decide what you need to do next to take the learning forward.

The responsive adult (see page 5)

In three interconnecting roles, the responsive adult will be:

* observing
* listening
* interpreting

observer

* **modelling**
* **playing alongside**
* **offering suggestions**
* **responding sensitively**
* **initiating with care!**

co-player

* discussing ideas
* sharing thinking
* modelling new skills
* asking open questions
* being an informed extender
* instigating ideas and thoughts
* supporting children as they make links in learning
* making possibilities evident
* introducing new ideas and resources
* offering challenges and provocations

extender

Offering challenges and provocations - some ideas:

NOTE: Soap and wax have similar properties, and can both be carved, using small knives, such as butter knives, or spoons, sharp sticks or pencils. Offer children bargain shop candles, and market stall soap to experiment with, before giving them more complex provocations and challenges.

? Find some candles. Can you:
  * carve them into spirals;
  * carve them into cubes or a cuboids;
  * make name candles, with your own name on;
  * make candle rulers with measurements down the sides;
  * carve them into a sculpture of a pen or pencil;
  * make decorated candles with lines, spots or scratches;
  * stick on objects such as ribbons, leaves, buttons, sequins or beads.

? Use recycled materials to make a celebration holder for night lights or floating candles, and decorate it with found objects.

? Find some bars of soap and soak them in warm water for an hour. What happens? Take a photo of the wet soap.

? What can you do with your soap now? Can you mould it or make it a different shape? See what you can do, and take photos of your creations. What happens to the wet soap creations as they dry?

? Put some birthday candles or wax crayons in a container and put the container somewhere warm (on a radiator, in bright sunshine or in a very low oven). What happens to the wax? Can you change the shape of the crayons or candles now? If you can, make some different shapes that can stand up or hang on a mobile.

? Can you write some secret messages or pictures using white candles to write with. How will your friends know how to see the message?

Ready for more?

- Find some bars of soap and use teaspoons, forks or clay tools to carve patterns in the soap. Look on Google Images 'soap carving' for ideas.

- Collect up as many old wax crayon ends as you can (ask in Reception as well as Year 1 and Year 2). Now ask an adult to help you to melt the crayons in a jam tart tray. You can sort the crayons into colours or make mixed creations. How can you use your new recycled crayons?

- Get a grater and grate some crayons or candles. How can you use the grated wax? http://daycaredaze.wordpress.com/2007/02/14/valentine-craft/ will give you one idea. If you grate soap, can you stick it back together again?

- Look at http://www.grandandtoy.ca/education/en/pro-melt.asp and find out how to do melted wax pictures.

- Can you use some bars of soap to make personalised gifts? You could cut or scratch signs of the zodiac, favourite objects, football badges or illuminated initials by using spoons, nails or screws to make the images. Find the designs you need in Google Images.

- White soap is really good for making polar bears. Research polar bear images on Google and see if you can make one of your own from a bar of soap. Take photos of the stages of the carving.

Materials, equipment suppliers, websites, books and other references

Try these ideas for free or cheap resources for soap and wax carving:
- bulk buy white kitchen candles;
- offer children tea lights (available in big bags from Ikea) for little or first carving experiences;
- ask parents and colleagues for part-used or unwanted decorative candles;
- buy tablets of bargain soap from supermarkets and market stalls;
- look in sales for decorative candles that may have been slightly damaged.

Tools don't need to be expensive. Collect some of these:
- old teaspoons;
- blunt knives;
- potato peelers;
- cocktail sticks;
- nails and screws.

Some websites

www.associatedcontent.com/article/133198/soap_carving_you_can_do_with_children.html - a 'how to' article.

www.flyingpigs.org.uk/crafts/Soap_Carving.pdf - to download a useful pdf of instructions on soap carving

http://www.workshopnetwork.co.uk/search/details.asp?Artist=355 and artists' workshop with pictures of children making wire, soap and mud sculptures.

www.hitentertainment.com/artattacK/ - the Art Attack site with lots of activities including soap carving, sponge sculptures etc

Google Images 'soap carving' 'wax carving' 'candles' 'decorative candles' 'candle art' 'soap art'.

Book

Soap Carving: For Children of All Ages; Howard K. Suzuki; Schiffer Publishing

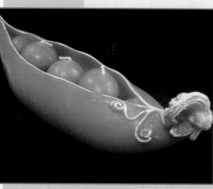

Curriculum coverage grid overleaf

Potential NC KS1 Curriculum Coverage through the provocations suggested for wax and soap.

Full version of KS1 PoS on pages 69-74
Photocopiable version on page 8

Literacy	Lit 1 speak	Lit 2 listen	Lit 3 group	Lit 4 drama	Lit 5 word	Lit 6 spell	Lit 7 text1	Lit 8 text2	Lit 9 text3	Lit10 text4	Lit11 sentence	Lit12 presentation
	1.1	2.1	3.1	4.1	5.1	6.1	7.1	8.1	9.1	10.1	11.1	12.1
	1.2	2.2	3.2	4.2	5.2	6.2	7.2	8.2	9.2	10.2	11.2	12.2

Numeracy	Num 1 U&A	Num 2 count	Num 3 number	Num 4 calculate	Num 5 shape	Num 6 measure	Num 7 data
	1.1	2.1	3.1	4.1	5.1	6.1	7.1
	1.2	2.2	3.2	4.2	5.2	6.2	7.2

Science	SC1 Enquiry			SC2 Life processes					SC3 Materials		SC4 Phys processes		
	Sc1.1	Sc1.2	Sc1.3	Sc2.1	Sc2.2	Sc2.3	Sc2.4	Sc2.5	Sc3.1	Sc3.2	Sc4.1	Sc4.2	Sc4.3
	1.1a	1.2a	1.3a	2.1a	2.2a	2.3a	2.4a	2.5a	3.1a	3.2a	4.1a	4.2a	4.3a
	1.1b	1.2b	1.3b	2.1b	2.2b	2.3b	2.4b	2.5b	3.1b	3.2b	4.1b	4.2b	4.3b
	1.1c	1.2c	1.3c	2.1c	2.2c	2.3c		2.5c	3.1c		4.1c	4.2c	4.3c
	1.1d				2.2d				3.1d				4.3d
					2.2e								
					2.2f								
					2.2g								

History	H1 chronology	H2 events, people	H3 interpret	H4 enquire	H5 org & comm	H6 breadth
	1a	2a	3a	4a	5a	6a
	1b	2b		4b		6b
						6c
						6d

Geography	G1.1 & G1.2 enquiry		G2 places	G3 processes	G4 environment	G5 breadth
	1.1a	1.2a	2a	3a	4a	5a
	1.1b	1.2b	2b	3b	4b	5b
	1.1c	1.2c	2c			5c
	1.1d	1.2d	2d			5d
			2e			

PHSE & C	PSHEC1 conf & resp	PSHEC2 citizenship	PSHEC3 health	PSHEC4 relationships
	1a	2a	3a	4a
	1b	2b	3b	4b
	1c	2c	3c	4c
	1d	2d	3d	4d
	1e	2e	3e	4e
		2f	3f	
		2g	3g	
		2h		

ICT	ICT 1 finding out	ICT 2 ideas	ICT 3 reviewing	ICT 4 breadth
	1.1a	1.2a	2a	3a	4a
	1.1b	1.2b	2b	3b	4b
	1.1c	1.2c		3c	4c
		1.2d			

D&T	D&T 1 developing	D&T 2 tool use	D&T 3 evaluating	D&T 4 materials	D&T 5 breadth
	1a	2a	3a	4a	5a
	1b	2b	3b	4b	5b
	1c	2c			5c
	1d	2d			
	1e	2e			

Music	M1 performing	M2 composing	M3 appraising	M4 listening	M5 breadth
	1a	2a	3a	4a	5a
	1b	2b	3b	4b	5b
	1c			4c	5c
					5d

Art & Design	A&D1 ideas	A&D2 making	A&D3 evaluating	A&D4 materials	A&D5 breadth
	1a	2a	3a	4a	5a
	1b	2b	3b	4b	5b
		2c		4c	5c
					5d

PE	PE1 devel skills	PE2 apply skills	PE3 evaluate	PE4 fitness	PE5 breadth
	1a	2a	3a	4a	5a dance
	1b	2b	3b	4b	5b games
		2c	3c		5c gym

Critical skills	Thinking Skills
problem solving	observing
decision making	classifying
critical thinking	prediction
creative thinking	making inferences
communication	problem solving
organisation	drawing conclusions
management	
leadership	

Shaving Foam and Spray Cream

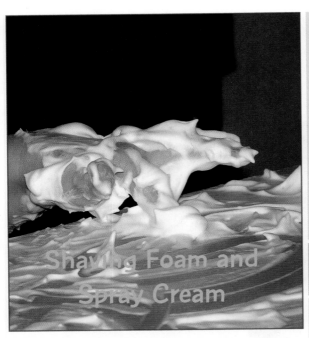

Shaving Foam and Spray Cream

Previous experience in the Foundation Stage

Throughout their time in the EYFS, most children will have played with shaving foam as part of messy play. They may have:

* used shaving foam for mark making on table tops or in trays;
* added different substances to shaving foam, such as lentils, paint, sand, glitter;
* manipulated shaving foam underneath cling film or in zip-lock bags;
* experimented with making simple temporary sculptures using the foam.

If your children have not played with shaving foam, give them some of these free play experiences before expecting them to concentrate on challenges!

Pause for thought

In the early stages of working with these materials it is crucial to continue to observe the children. Only by doing this can you set developmentally appropriate challenges and provocations. The ideas listed here are offered as suggestions; the most exciting challenges will arise from children's own interests and motivations, which will only become apparent as you spend time with them, watching and joining them in their play. As you do this, you will be moving between the three interconnecting roles of observer, co-player, extender described below, and will be able to decide what you need to do next to take the learning forward.

The responsive adult (see page 5)

In three interconnecting roles, the responsive adult will be:

* observing
* listening
* interpreting

observer

* **modelling**
* **playing alongside**
* **offering suggestions**
* **responding sensitively**
* **initiating with care!**

co-player

* discussing ideas
* sharing thinking
* modelling new skills
* asking open questions
* being an informed extender
* instigating ideas and thoughts
* supporting children as they make links in learning
* making possibilities evident
* introducing new ideas and resources
* offering challenges and provocations

extender

Offering challenges and provocations - some ideas:

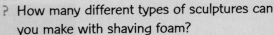
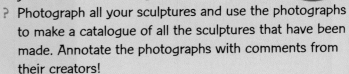

NOTE: Make sure you have a camera handy when you offer these resources - sculptures made from foam are short-lived!

? How many different types of sculptures can you make with shaving foam?

? Photograph all your sculptures and use the photographs to make a catalogue of all the sculptures that have been made. Annotate the photographs with comments from their creators!

? Can you make a range of monsters, vehicles or some other theme and photograph your sculptures to make a book? Perhaps some of your creations could form the basis for a story or a poem?

? What is the biggest sculpture that you can make with shaving foam?

? Make lists of important vocabulary or key words in shaving foam. Photograph them for a wall display.

? Try adding powder or ready-mixed paint, glitter and other substances to your foam to create interesting effects.

? Can you create a 'set' or habitat for some small word characters? Try adding leaves, twigs, bark, flowers and other interesting materials?

? Make a range of pretend pies. How many different ways can you find of decorating them?

? Try doing some mathematical calculations with shaving foam!

? What happens when you leave a foam sculpture for some time, such as a couple of days? Can you take a series of photos or make some drawings to show what happens? Use the photos or drawings to make a flick book, so you can speed up the process.

Ready for more?

- Make some 'combs' from stiff plastic or card (cut some plastic from empty washing-up liquid bottles and flatten it somewhere warm before cutting your combs out). Try the combs out in shaving foam to see what effects you can create. Try forks, kitchen implements and sieves as well.

- Hide things in the shaving foam for your friends to find. Once everything has been found, count, classify, and graph the items.

- Try marbling with shaving foam. Put about an inch of foam in the bottom of a plastic tray. Use your hand or a piece of card to smooth it out. Now put some water colour paint into a spray bottle and spray colour on to the foam. (Three colours is usually sufficient.) You can then use a paintbrush to pull the colour through the foam. Finally, lay a piece of paper on top of the foam and rub gently to transfer the pattern.

- Use the above process, but instead of using water colour use fabric paint. Then you can transfer the design to fabric.

- Experiment with whisks in warm water with washing-up liquid. See how many bubbles you can make. Colour the foam with food colouring. Or you could blow the bubbles for foam by using a straw in a mixture of water, food colouring and washing-up liquid or bubble liquid.

Materials, equipment suppliers, websites, books and other references

Shaving foam is a very inexpensive resource for manipulating and temporary construction. It is easy to use, has very calming effects on some children, and really helps with fine motor skills, as well as creativity. Spray cream is an alternative for the same activities described here, particularly for children who may be allergic to shaving foam.

Get shaving foam from:

- bargain chemists or 'pound' shops. Try to get non-allergenic, perfume free varieties.
- children really don't need tools for this activity, but you could offer spoons, spatulas, scoops and brushes if you wish. Table tops of builders' trays are suitable surfaces for free play. For individual work, offer baking trays, flat plastic containers or lids from ice cream tubs.
- additions to foam play could include paint, food colouring, aromatherapy oils, glitter or sequins.
- encourage children to collect and add natural materials such as twigs, flowers or leaves. They may also add small world animals and toys, toy cars or superhero and fantasy figures.

Or you can make your own foam by whisking soapy water with hand whisks.

Put 'foam city' in Google Web or Google Images for a great video sequence of a street full of foam.

Some books:

The Little Book of Messy Play; Sally Featherstone; Featherstone Education
The Little Book of Mark Making; Sam Goodman; Featherstone Education
Children's Arts and Crafts and *More Children's Arts and Crafts*; Australian Women's Weekly
Primary Art and *Messy Art*; Mary Ann Kohl; Brilliant Publications
Adventurous Art; Susan Milford; Williamson
Mudworks; Mary Ann Kohl; Bright Ring

Curriculum coverage grid overleaf

Potential NC KS1 Curriculum Coverage through the provocations suggested for shaving foam & cream.

Literacy

	Lit 1 speak	Lit 2 listen	Lit 3 group	Lit 4 drama	Lit 5 word	Lit 6 spell	Lit 7 text1	Lit 8 text2	Lit 9 text3	Lit10 text4	Lit11 sentence	Lit12 presentation
Literacy	1.1	2.1	3.1	4.1	5.1	6.1	7.1	8.1	9.1	10.1	11.1	12.1
	1.2	2.2	3.2	4.2	5.2	6.2	7.2	8.2	9.2	10.2	11.2	12.2

Numeracy

Full version of KS1 PoS on pages 69-74
Photocopiable version on page 8

	Num 1 U&A	Num 2 count	Num 3 number	Num 4 calculate	Num 5 shape	Num 6 measure	Num 7 data
Numeracy	1.1	2.1	3.1	4.1	5.1	6.1	7.1
	1.2	2.2	3.2	4.2	5.2	6.2	7.2

Science

	SC1 Enquiry			SC2 Life processes					SC3 Materials		SC4 Phys processes		
	Sc1.1	Sc1.2	Sc1.3	Sc2.1	Sc2.2	Sc2.3	Sc2.4	Sc2.5	Sc3.1	Sc3.2	Sc4.1	Sc4.2	Sc4.3
Science	1.1a	1.2a	1.3a	2.1a	2.2a	2.3a	2.4a	2.5a	3.1a	3.2a	4.1a	4.2a	4.3a
	1.1b	1.2b	1.3b	2.1b	2.2b	2.3b	2.4b	2.5b	3.1b	3.2b	4.1b	4.2b	4.3b
	1.1c	1.2c	1.3c	2.1c	2.2c	2.3c		2.5c	3.1c		4.1c	4.2c	4.3c
	1.1d				2.2d				3.1d				4.3d
					2.2e								
					2.2f								
					2.2g								

ICT

	ICT 1 finding out	ICT 2 ideas	ICT 3 reviewing	ICT 4 breadth
ICT	1.1a 1.2a	2a	3a	4a
	1.1b 1.2b	2b	3b	4b
	1.1c 1.2c		3c	4c
	1.2d			

D&T

	D&T 1 developing	D&T 2 tool use	D&T 3 evaluating	D&T 4 materials	D&T 5 breadth
D&T	1a	2a	3a	4a	5a
	1b	2b	3b	4b	5b
	1c	2c			5c
	1d	2d			
	1e	2e			

History

	H1 chronology	H2 events, people	H3 interpret	H4 enquire	H5 org & comm	H6 breadth
History	1a	2a	3a	4a	5a	6a
	1b	2b		4b		6b
						6c
						6d

Geography

	G1.1 & G1.2 enquiry		G2 places	G3 processes	G4 environment	G5 breadth
Geography	1.1a	1.2a	2a	3a	4a	5a
	1.1b	1.2b	2b	3b	4b	5b
	1.1c	1.2c	2c			5c
	1.1d	1.2d	2d			5d
			2e			

Music

	M1 performing	M2 composing	M3 appraising	M4 listening	M5 breadth
Music	1a	2a	3a	4a	5a
	1b	2b	3b	4b	5b
	1c			4c	5c
					5d

PHSE & C

	PSHEC1 conf & resp	PSHEC2 citizenship	PSHEC3 health	PSHEC4 relationships
PHSE & C	1a	2a	3a	4a
	1b	2b	3b	4b
	1c	2c	3c	4c
	1d	2d	3d	4d
	1e	2e	3e	4e
		2f	3f	
		2g	3g	
		2h		

Art & Design

	A&D1 ideas	A&D2 making	A&D3 evaluating	A&D4 materials	A&D5 breadth
Art & Design	1a	2a	3a	4a	5a
	1b	2b	3b	4b	5b
		2c		4c	5c
					5d

PE

	PE1 devel skills	PE2 apply skills	PE3 evaluate	PE4 fitness	PE5 breadth
PE	1a	2a	3a	4a	5a dance
	1b	2b	3b	4b	5b games
		2c	3c		5c gym

Critical skills	Thinking Skills
problem solving	observing
decision making	classifying
critical thinking	prediction
creative thinking	making inferences
communication	problem solving
organisation	drawing conclusions
management	
leadership	

Fruit and Vegetables

Fruit and Vegetables

Previous experience in the Foundation Stage

During their time in the Foundation Stage most children will have worked with fruit and vegetables in a variety of ways. They may have:

* printed with potatoes and other vegetables, drawn these objects and made close observations of their features;
* made soups and stews, cutting up and looking at vegetables;
* prepared a variety of fruit and vegetables for snack time, including fruit kebabs, fruit jellies, individual pizzas;
* played with fruit and vegetables as part of home corner play;
* been involved in visiting the greengrocers to buy fruit and vegetables, or grown their own.

Pause for thought

In the early stages of working with these materials it is crucial to continue to observe the children. Only by doing this can you set developmentally appropriate challenges and provocations. The ideas listed here are offered as suggestions; the most exciting challenges will arise from children's own interests and motivations, which will only become apparent as you spend time with them, watching and joining them in their play. As you do this, you will be moving between the three interconnecting roles of observer, co-player, extender described below, and will be able to decide what you need to do next to take the learning forward.

The responsive adult (see page 5)

In three interconnecting roles, the responsive adult will be:

* observing
* listening
* interpreting

* **modelling**
* **playing alongside**
* **offering suggestions**
* **responding sensitively**
* **initiating with care!**

* discussing ideas
* sharing thinking
* modelling new skills
* asking open questions
* being an informed extender
* instigating ideas and thoughts
* supporting children as they make links in learning
* making possibilities evident
* introducing new ideas and resources
* offering challenges and provocations

Offering challenges and provocations - some ideas:

Experience of looking at and using fruit and vegetables decoratively in cooking and other food preparation will give children a knowledge to build on as they take on more complex challenges.

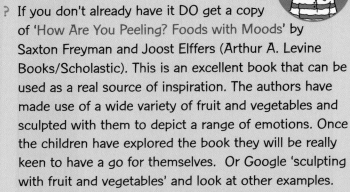

? If you don't already have it DO get a copy of 'How Are You Peeling? Foods with Moods' by Saxton Freyman and Joost Elffers (Arthur A. Levine Books/Scholastic). This is an excellent book that can be used as a real source of inspiration. The authors have made use of a wide variety of fruit and vegetables and sculpted with them to depict a range of emotions. Once the children have explored the book they will be really keen to have a go for themselves. Or Google 'sculpting with fruit and vegetables' and look at other examples.

? Can you use fruit and vegetable to make characters that are, for example, angry, disappointed, excited, nervous, sad? Can you photograph your characters to make your own book of Foods with Moods?

? Can you make some fruit and vegetable characters and write a story for them? Can you illustrate your story with photographs of your characters? You could make the 'Potato Family,' Carrot Family,' 'Parsnip Family,' etc.

? Can you squeeze some juices to make smoothies from your fruit and vegetables? Try different flavours and combinations and hold a survey to find which are most popular. Graph the results. Set up a Smoothie Bar and write a menu of all the different drinks available. Invite other children or parents to a Smoothie party.

? Make your own recipe book of smoothies you have designed.

? Can you make some fruit kebabs? Experiment with fruits, colours and patterns to make new combinations.

Ready for more?

♻ Choose a traditional tale, for example *The Three Little Pigs.* Can you make the characters out of fruit and vegetables?

♻ Can you create fillings for stuffing tomatoes, mushrooms, peppers and apples? Try them out on your friends. Which are the most popular?

♻ Google *Pumpkin Lanterns.* Can you create some pumpkin lanterns? Can you make lanterns from any other fruit and vegetables?

♻ Can you create fillings for lettuce and cabbage leaves, or vine leaves?

♻ Can you create your own recipe book for stuffed fruit and vegetables? Use photographs of your own creations as a basis for the book. Get your friends to write reviews of your creations.

♻ Can you make a sorbet with an orange or a lemon and serve it in the original skin?

♻ Can you make a pomander using oranges or lemons? How many different ways can you find to decorate it?

♻ Get some dried peas and soak them overnight in water. Now use the peas and some cocktail sticks to make some sculptures. You could try adding chick-peas or other dried beans or seeds. What sorts of sculptures can you make? Can you make these objects into a ball struc-ture, or a tower?

Materials, equipment suppliers, websites, books and other references

Fruit and vegetables are cheap resources for art work and construction. Ask local greengrocers or market traders for any bargains they may have, and remember that potatoes, turnips, carrots and swede are cheap basic ingredients., If you have a problem with working with food, use the vegetables for soup after the children have made their creations.

For some more unusual creations try:
* packets of vine leaves;
* peppers and aubergines;
* pot pourri;
* dried peas or tinned chick peas with cocktail sticks;
* add 'googly eyes', beads, sequins, mapping pins, wire.

Collect some baskets or boxes of stones, leaves, nuts, feathers, cones and other natural objects - keep these fresh by removing the old ones and replacing with collections from walks, visits, holidays and so on. Always encourage children to pick up natural materials for the collection, and ask them to bring a shell, pebble, cone, leaf or a piece of driftwood from their holidays and you'll soon have a collection! The message about collecting natural objects should always be **'If it isn't fixed on, it is likely to be OK. If it is fixed on - ask!'** Buy pot pourri, polished pebbles, glass beads from bargain shops. Ask local florists or market traders for 'past their sell by' flowers to use for Rangoli and other art works.

Look up **'Rangoli'** on the internet and find out about this form of art, originally found on doorsteps. You can also download versions of rangoli patterns to use as bases for your creations with real petals, leaves, sand etc. Try www.activityvillage.co.uk/rangoli.htm or http://www.ehow.com/

This site has pattern templates to download - http://www.dltk-kids.com/World/india/mrangoli.htm

Try **Google Images**: 'natural art' 'art from nature' 'Andy Goldsworthy' 'natural collage' 'pebble art' 'painted stone' 'rangoli' 'petals' 'leaves'.

Books:

Nature Crafts for Kids; Gwen Diehn; Sterling Juvenile;

Arts in the School Grounds; Brian Keaney; Learning Through Landscapes

Hands-on Nature; Jenepher Lingelbach; University Press of New England

Nature's Playground; Fiona Danks; Frances Lincoln

Ecoart!; Lauri Carlson; Williamson Publishing

Potential NC KS1 Curriculum Coverage through the provocations suggested for fruit and vegetables.

Literacy

Literacy	Lit 1 speak	Lit 2 listen	Lit 3 group	Lit 4 drama	Lit 5 word	Lit 6 spell	Lit 7 text1	Lit 8 text2	Lit 9 text3	Lit10 text4	Lit11 sentence	Lit12 presentation
	1.1	2.1	3.1	4.1	5.1	6.1	7.1	8.1	9.1	10.1	11.1	12.1
	1.2	2.2	3.2	4.2	5.2	6.2	7.2	8.2	9.2	10.2	11.2	12.2

Numeracy

Numeracy	Num 1 U&A	Num 2 count	Num 3 number	Num 4 calculate	Num 5 shape	Num 6 measure	Num 7 data
	1.1	2.1	3.1	4.1	5.1	6.1	7.1
	1.2	2.2	3.2	4.2	5.2	6.2	7.2

Full version of KS1 PoS on pages 69-74
Photocopiable version on page 8

Science

Science	SC1 Enquiry			SC2 Life processes					SC3 Materials		SC4 Phys processes		
	Sc1.1	Sc1.2	Sc1.3	Sc2.1	Sc2.2	Sc2.3	Sc2.4	Sc2.5	Sc3.1	Sc3.2	Sc4.1	Sc4.2	Sc4.3
	1.1a	1.2a	1.3a	2.1a	2.2a	2.3a	2.4a	2.5a	3.1a	3.2a	4.1a	4.2a	4.3a
	1.1b	1.2b	1.3b	2.1b	2.2b	2.3b	2.4b	2.5b	3.1b	3.2b	4.1b	4.2b	4.3b
	1.1c	1.2c	1.3c	2.1c	2.2c	2.3c		2.5c	3.1c		4.1c	4.2c	4.3c
	1.1d				2.2d				3.1d				4.3d
					2.2e								
					2.2f								
					2.2g								

ICT

ICT	ICT 1 finding out		ICT 2 ideas	ICT 3 reviewing	ICT 4 breadth
	1.1a	1.2a	2a	3a	4a
	1.1b	1.2b	2b	3b	4b
	1.1c	1.2c		3c	4c
		1.2d			

D&T

D&T	D&T 1 developing	D&T 2 tool use	D&T 3 evaluating	D&T 4 materials	D&T 5 breadth
	1a	2a	3a	4a	5a
	1b	2b	3b	4b	5b
	1c	2c			5c
	1d	2d			
	1e	2e			

History

History	H1 chronology	H2 events, people	H3 interpret	H4 enquire	H5 org & comm	H6 breadth
	1a	2a	3a	4a	5a	6a
	1b	2b		4b		6b
						6c
						6d

Geography

Geography	G1.1 & G1.2 enquiry		G2 places	G3 processes	G4 environment	G5 breadth
	1.1a	1.2a	2a	3a	4a	5a
	1.1b	1.2b	2b	3b	4b	5b
	1.1c	1.2c	2c			5c
	1.1d	1.2d	2d			5d
			2e			

Music

Music	M1 performing	M2 composing	M3 appraising	M4 listening	M5 breadth
	1a	2a	3a	4a	5a
	1b	2b	3b	4b	5b
	1c			4c	5c
					5d

PHSE & C

PHSE & C	PSHEC1 conf & resp	PSHEC2 citizenship	PSHEC3 health	PSHEC4 relationships
	1a	2a	3a	4a
	1b	2b	3b	4b
	1c	2c	3c	4c
	1d	2d	3d	4d
	1e	2e	3e	4e
		2f	3f	
		2g	3g	
		2h		

Art & Design

Art & Design	A&D1 ideas	A&D2 making	A&D3 evaluating	A&D4 materials	A&D5 breadth
	1a	2a	3a	4a	5a
	1b	2b	3b	4b	5b
		2c		4c	5c
					5d

PE

PE	PE1 devel skills	PE2 apply skills	PE3 evaluate	PE4 fitness	PE5 breadth
	1a	2a	3a	4a	5a dance
	1b	2b	3b	4b	5b games
		2c	3c		5c gym

Critical skills	Thinking Skills
problem solving	observing
decision making	classifying
critical thinking	prediction
creative thinking	making inferences
communication	problem solving
organisation	drawing conclusions
management	
leadership	

Stuffing

Stuffing

Previous experience in the Foundation Stage
While in the EYFS most children will have spent time stuffing things inside other things as part of schematic play. All early years practitioners will be familiar with the child who takes a bag into the home corner and stuffs it full with the resources that the other children are trying to play with! Children may also have:
* stuffed paper bags or socks to make simple puppets;
* stuffed old clothes to make a Guy Fawkes or other figures;
* stuffed various containers with newspaper and other materials as part of their free play in the workshop area.

Pause for thought
In the early stages of working with these materials it is crucial to continue to observe the children. Only by doing this can you set developmentally appropriate challenges and provocations. The ideas listed here are offered as suggestions; the most exciting challenges will arise from children's own interests and motivations, which will only become apparent as you spend time with them, watching and joining them in their play. As you do this, you will be moving between the three interconnecting roles of observer, co-player, extender described below, and will be able to decide what you need to do next to take the learning forward.

The responsive adult (see page 5)
In three interconnecting roles, the responsive adult will be:

observer
* observing
* listening
* interpreting

co-player
* **modelling**
* **playing alongside**
* **offering suggestions**
* **responding sensitively**
* **initiating with care!**

extender
* discussing ideas
* sharing thinking
* modelling new skills
* asking open questions
* being an informed extender
* instigating ideas and thoughts
* supporting children as they make links in learning
* making possibilities evident
* introducing new ideas and resources
* offering challenges and provocations

Offering challenges and provocations - some ideas:

NOTE: Enclosing something inside something else is a concept that pre-occupies many pre-school children and it is usually possible to find a few children in Year 1 for whom enclosing is still important:

? How many different materials can you identify that would be suitable for stuffing things? Work with your friends to make a list, then collect some of the materials and experiment.
? Can you design or think of some characters that could be made by stuffing old clothes?
? How many different ways can you find to make the hands/body/face for a stuffed character?
? Once you have made your characters, can you write an adventure story for them? Perhaps you could take photographs to illustrate your story and make a Power Point presentation.
? How many different things can you make by stuffing old tights, for example, could you make a beanstalk for a role play of *Jack and the Beanstalk*, or a sea serpent for a pirate story?
? What is the longest creature you can make? Can you find out how long the Loch Ness Monster is thought to be?
? Can you make some scary monsters by stuffing old tights? Use string, wire, buttons, sequins, metal objects to help make your creations more interesting!
? Can you make some puppet characters from old socks? How many different types of creatures can you make? Why not make a puppet theatre by hanging a piece of fabric from hooks halfway up the frame of a door. Now write a play for your characters and invite some other children to watch.
? Can you make your own stuffed toy? It can be any sort, even a creature that has never existed.

Ready for more?

- Design and make some doorstops or draugh stoppers. What will you put inside them to make them heavy enough to hold a door open or keep out a real draught? Google 'fabric doorstop' or 'draught stopper' for some ideas.

- Can you make a collection of unwanted soft toys and turn them into doorstops by undoing a seam and placing something heavy inside?

- Try stuffing some vegetables. Which vegetables are best for stuffing and what ingredients would be good? Can you find some recipes or make up some of your own? See if you can get hold of a marrow and invent some recipes for stuffed marrow. Try your stuffed vegetables out on your friends and make a graph to show which recipes are the most popular!

- Can you make your own bean bags and invent some games to play with them?

- Make your own cushion or pillow.

- Can you make some 'smelly bags' by stuffing material with flowers or herbs?

- Design and make a bed for a pet?

- Instead of putting stuffing into something, why not try taking the stuffing OUT of some old stuffed toys so that you can turn them into puppets! Make sure you ask first!

Materials, equipment suppliers, websites, books and other references

Sources:

If you want to buy new wadding, try:

www.hobbycraft.co.uk/ideas_library/idea_87.html - for filling for toys and a reindeer draught stopper.

Other materials for stuffing toys and simple items are plentiful and cheap. Try:

- sheep's wool collected from hedges and fences;
- torn-up fabric;
- paper shreddings;
- polystyrene beads or 'wiggles';
- newspaper;
- hay or straw;
- cotton wool;
- cotton wadding.

There are lots of ideas on the Internet for simple stuffing activities to make toys and other items. Try:

* http://rubyglen.com/crafts/snowman.htm for a simple snowman doorstop
* http://www.thriftyfun.com/tf957998.tip.html for draught stoppers made from socks
* http://jas.familyfun.go.com/arts-and-crafts?page=CraftDisplay&craftid=11565 for draught stoppers

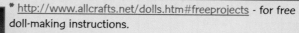

* http://www.allcrafts.net/dolls.htm#freeprojects - for free doll-making instructions.

Use **Google Images** for pictures - some suggestions for words to search: 'stuffed toys' 'stuffed animals' 'soft toys'.

Some **books and stories**:

Dogger; Shirley Hughes; Red Fox

Stupid Sock Creatures; Making Quirky, Lovable Figures from Cast-off Socks; John Murphy; Lark Books

Bean Bag Toys: Kathryn Severns; KP Books

Easy-to-Make Stuffed Dinosaurs; Zillah Halls; Dover

Make Your Own Teddy Bears and Bear Clothes (Quick Starts for Kids!); Jodie Davis; Williamson

Make Your Own Toys (Recyling Fun); Five Mile Press

Curriculum coverage grid overleaf

Potential NC KS1 Curriculum Coverage through the provocations suggested for stuffing.

Full version of KS1 PoS on pages 69-74
Photocopiable version on page 8

Literacy

	Lit 1 speak	Lit 2 listen	Lit 3 group	Lit 4 drama	Lit 5 word	Lit 6 spell	Lit 7 text1	Lit 8 text2	Lit 9 text3	Lit10 text4	Lit11 sentence	Lit12 presentation
Literacy	1.1	2.1	3.1	4.1	5.1	6.1	7.1	8.1	9.1	10.1	11.1	12.1
	1.2	2.2	3.2	4.2	5.2	6.2	7.2	8.2	9.2	10.2	11.2	12.2

Numeracy

	Num 1 U&A	Num 2 count	Num 3 number	Num 4 calculate	Num 5 shape	Num 6 measure	Num 7 data
Numeracy	1.1	2.1	3.1	4.1	5.1	6.1	7.1
	1.2	2.2	3.2	4.2	5.2	6.2	7.2

Science

	SC1 Enquiry			SC2 Life processes					SC3 Materials		SC4 Phys processes		
	Sc1.1	Sc1.2	Sc1.3	Sc2.1	Sc2.2	Sc2.3	Sc2.4	Sc2.5	Sc3.1	Sc3.2	Sc4.1	Sc4.2	Sc4.3
Science	1.1a	1.2a	1.3a	2.1a	2.2a	2.3a	2.4a	2.5a	3.1a	3.2a	4.1a	4.2a	4.3a
	1.1b	1.2b	1.3b	2.1b	2.2b	2.3b	2.4b	2.5b	3.1b	3.2b	4.1b	4.2b	4.3b
	1.1c	1.2c	1.3c	2.1c	2.2c	2.3c		2.5c	3.1c		4.1c	4.2c	4.3c
	1.1d				2.2d				3.1d				4.3d
					2.2e								
					2.2f								
					2.2g								

ICT

	ICT 1 finding out		ICT 2 ideas	ICT 3 reviewing	ICT 4 breadth
ICT	1.1a	1.2a	2a	3a	4a
	1.1b	1.2b	2b	3b	4b
	1.1c	1.2c		3c	4c
		1.2d			

History

	H1 chronology	H2 events, people	H3 interpret	H4 enquire	H5 org & comm	H6 breadth
History	1a	2a	3a	4a	5a	6a
	1b	2b		4b		6b
						6c
						6d

Geography

	G1.1 & G1.2 enquiry		G2 places	G3 processes	G4 environment	G5 breadth
Geography	1.1a	1.2a	2a	3a	4a	5a
	1.1b	1.2b	2b	3b	4b	5b
	1.1c	1.2c	2c			5c
	1.1d	1.2d	2d			5d
			2e			

D&T

	D&T 1 developing	D&T 2 tool use	D&T 3 evaluating	D&T 4 materials	D&T 5 breadth
D&T	1a	2a	3a	4a	5a
	1b	2b	3b	4b	5b
	1c	2c			5c
	1d	2d			
	1e	2e			

Music

	M1 performing	M2 composing	M3 appraising	M4 listening	M5 breadth
Music	1a	2a	3a	4a	5a
	1b	2b	3b	4b	5b
	1c			4c	5c
					5d

PHSE & C

	PSHEC1 conf & resp	PSHEC2 citizenship	PSHEC3 health	PSHEC4 relationships
PHSE & C	1a	2a	3a	4a
	1b	2b	3b	4b
	1c	2c	3c	4c
	1d	2d	3d	4d
	1e	2e	3e	4e
		2f	3f	
		2g	3g	
		2h		

Art & Design

	A&D1 ideas	A&D2 making	A&D3 evaluating	A&D4 materials	A&D5 breadth
Art & Design	1a	2a	3a	4a	5a
	1b	2b	3b	4b	5b
		2c		4c	5c
					5d

PE

	PE1 devel skills	PE2 apply skills	PE3 evaluate	PE4 fitness	PE5 breadth
PE	1a	2a	3a	4a	5a dance
	1b	2b	3b	4b	5b games
		2c	3c		5c gym

Critical skills	Thinking Skills
problem solving	observing
decision making	classifying
critical thinking	prediction
creative thinking	making inferences
communication	problem solving
organisation	drawing conclusions
management	
leadership	

Moulding

Moulding

Previous experience in the Foundation Stage

Children may have already had experience of moulding with play resources in the following ways:

* using sand moulds for mud, sand, or compost;
* using moulds for jellies and other foods;
* moulding clay or dough;
* moulding other malleable materials such as paper pulp;
* looking at footprints and other marks in mud, sand etc.

Pause for thought

In the early stages of working with these materials it is crucial to continue to observe the children. Only by doing this can you set developmentally appropriate challenges and provocations. The ideas listed here are offered as suggestions; the most exciting challenges will arise from children's own interests and motivations, which will only become apparent as you spend time with them, watching and joining them in their play. As you do this, you will be moving between the three interconnecting roles of observer, co-player, extender described below, and will be able to decide what you need to do next to take the learning forward.

The responsive adult (see page 5)

In three interconnecting roles, the responsive adult will be:

* observing
* listening
* interpreting

observer

* **modelling**
* **playing alongside**
* **offering suggestions**
* **responding sensitively**
* **initiating with care!**

co-player

* discussing ideas
* sharing thinking
* modelling new skills
* asking open questions
* being an informed extender
* instigating ideas and thoughts
* supporting children as they make links in learning
* making possibilities evident
* introducing new ideas and resources
* offering challenges and provocations

extender

Offering challenges and provocations - some ideas:

Children will almost certainly have used manufactured moulds for sand and dough. They may never have thought about how to make moulds from familiar objects, or using one object to make a mould for multiple objects. Give older children plenty of time to experience and discuss activities which build on their earlier knowledge.

? Use some sand or dough moulds to make shapes in sand, dough or mud. How do moulds work?

? Can you make a mould from recycled materials? You could try some of these:
  * the insides from chocolate or sweet boxes;
  * cups of all sorts, including paper and plastic cups;
  * foil cases from jam tarts and pies;
  * areosol, bottle and tin lids;
  * buckets, plastic boxes, egg cartons.

Try your moulds with sand, dough or mud, or fill them with water and freeze them.

? Tear some strips of newspaper and try pasting them over a mould such as:
  * a balloon;
  * a plastic bowl;
  * a plastic toy such as a big dinosaur figure;
  * a wellington boot;
  * a cardboard box.

Keep pasting layers until the structure is firm, and leave to dry. Now work out a way to get the paper shape off the mould. You may have to cut it. Look inside the paper mould, what can you see?

? Use jelly moulds to make jellies, blancmange or ice sculptures from coloured water.

? Get some shallow tin lids and bowls, and make bird food sculptures by filling the lids with bird seed, adding water and freezing overnight. Tip the ice sculptures out, leave them outside and watch the birds come to eat the seeds.

Ready for more?

- Find some small, clean things to use as moulds - you could use small cups or very clean yogurt pots. Fill these with cooked rice and make a healthy snack salad with shredded lettuce and rice castles, decorated with pieces of tomato, cucumber and cooked peas.
- If you enjoyed making bird food moulds, try making some bird cake. Look at http://www.rspb.org.uk/youth/makeanddo/activities/birdcake.asp to find out how to make bird cakes to hang outside in winter.
- Can you make a mould of a plastic animal, so you can make lots of copies? You need to choose a small model with a chunky body and short legs. Now try making a mould from sand or plaster. Once you have your mould, you will be able to make more copies of the animal.
- Make some healthy eating ice lollies. Use fruit juices and small pieces of fruit to fill ice lolly moulds. Freeze them and share them with you friends.
- Or make some savoury ice lollies from tomato juice, with peas, beans and small pieces of vegetable. Try these and see who likes them!
- Can you make a striped jelly or a rainbow jelly? Or can you make a jelly with real fruit pieces in it? Look at www.nigella.com/recipes for instructions, or 'rainbow jelly' in Google Images.

Materials, equipment suppliers, websites, books and other references

Resources:

Moulds can be made from lots of different items - it only needs a good imagination and lots of recycled containers:

- liners from chocolate and sweet boxes;
- bowls, mugs, cups and pots;
- jelly moulds from junk shops and rummage sales;
- plastic and polystyrene cups;
- boxes, packets, tins;
- plant pots and containers.

Use some of the following for moulding:

- cooked rice
- damp sand
- clay or mud
- dough or pastry
- jelly
- plaster or DIY filler
- aspic jelly (good for savoury moulds with vegetables set in them).

Google images: 'jelly mould' 'jelly baby' 'sandcastle' 'blancmange' 'giant jelly'
Google web search for information on suppliers of jelly moulds and party food making: http://www.jellyandblancmange.co.uk - has children's cooking equipment.

Books:

Don't Put Your Finger in the Jelly Nelly; Nick Sharratt; Scholastic
Developing Science in the Primary Classroom; Wynne Harlen; Longman
The Little Book of Science Through Art; Sally Featherstone; Featherstone Education
Guzzling Jelly with Giant Gorbelly; John Rice; Macmillan
Party Food; Sharon Dalgleish; Smart Apple Media

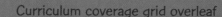
Curriculum coverage grid overleaf

Potential NC KS1 Curriculum Coverage through the provocations suggested for moulding.

Literacy

	Lit 1 speak	Lit 2 listen	Lit 3 group	Lit 4 drama	Lit 5 word	Lit 6 spell	Lit 7 text1	Lit 8 text2	Lit 9 text3	Lit10 text4	Lit11 sentence	Lit12 presentation
Literacy	1.1	2.1	3.1	4.1	5.1	6.1	7.1	8.1	9.1	10.1	11.1	12.1
	1.2	2.2	3.2	4.2	5.2	6.2	7.2	8.2	9.2	10.2	11.2	12.2

Numeracy

	Num 1 U&A	Num 2 count	Num 3 number	Num 4 calculate	Num 5 shape	Num 6 measure	Num 7 data
Numeracy	1.1	2.1	3.1	4.1	5.1	6.1	7.1
	1.2	2.2	3.2	4.2	5.2	6.2	7.2

Full version of KS1 PoS on pages 69-74
Photocopiable version on page 8

Science

	SC1 Enquiry			SC2 Life processes					SC3 Materials		SC4 Phys processes		
	Sc1.1	Sc1.2	Sc1.3	Sc2.1	Sc2.2	Sc2.3	Sc2.4	Sc2.5	Sc3.1	Sc3.2	Sc4.1	Sc4.2	Sc4.3
Science	1.1a	1.2a	1.3a	2.1a	2.2a	2.3a	2.4a	2.5a	3.1a	3.2a	4.1a	4.2a	4.3a
	1.1b	1.2b	1.3b	2.1b	2.2b	2.3b	2.4b	2.5b	3.1b	3.2b	4.1b	4.2b	4.3b
	1.1c	1.2c	1.3c	2.1c	2.2c	2.3c		2.5c	3.1c		4.1c	4.2c	4.3c
	1.1d				2.2d				3.1d				4.3d
					2.2e								
					2.2f								
					2.2g								

ICT

	ICT 1 finding out		ICT 2 ideas	ICT 3 reviewing	ICT 4 breadth
ICT	1.1a	1.2a	2a	3a	4a
	1.1b	1.2b	2b	3b	4b
	1.1c	1.2c		3c	4c
		1.2d			

D&T

	D&T 1 developing	D&T 2 tool use	D&T 3 evaluating	D&T 4 materials	D&T 5 breadth
D&T	1a	2a	3a	4a	5a
	1b	2b	3b	4b	5b
	1c	2c			5c
	1d	2d			
	1e	2e			

History

	H1 chronology	H2 events, people	H3 interpret	H4 enquire	H5 org & comm	H6 breadth
History	1a	2a	3a	4a	5a	6a
	1b	2b		4b		6b
						6c
						6d

Geography

	G1.1 & G1.2 enquiry		G2 places	G3 processes	G4 environment	G5 breadth
Geography	1.1a	1.2a	2a	3a	4a	5a
	1.1b	1.2b	2b	3b	4b	5b
	1.1c	1.2c	2c			5c
	1.1d	1.2d	2d			5d
			2e			

Music

	M1 performing	M2 composing	M3 appraising	M4 listening	M5 breadth
Music	1a	2a	3a	4a	5a
	1b	2b	3b	4b	5b
	1c			4c	5c
					5d

PHSE & C

	PSHEC1 conf & resp	PSHEC2 citizenship	PSHEC3 health	PSHEC4 relationships
PHSE & C	1a	2a	3a	4a
	1b	2b	3b	4b
	1c	2c	3c	4c
	1d	2d	3d	4d
	1e	2e	3e	4e
		2f	3f	
		2g	3g	
		2h		

Art & Design

	A&D1 ideas	A&D2 making	A&D3 evaluating	A&D4 materials	A&D5 breadth
Art & Design	1a	2a	3a	4a	5a
	1b	2b	3b	4b	5b
		2c		4c	5c
					5d

PE

	PE1 devel skills	PE2 apply skills	PE3 evaluate	PE4 fitness	PE5 breadth
PE	1a	2a	3a	4a	5a dance
	1b	2b	3b	4b	5b games
		2c	3c		5c gym

Critical skills	Thinking Skills
problem solving	observing
decision making	classifying
critical thinking	prediction
creative thinking	making inferences
communication	problem solving
organisation	drawing conclusions
management	
leadership	

Fabric

Fabric

Previous experience in the Foundation Stage

There will be very few children who will not, at some time in the EYFS, have used fabrics for different sorts of activities such as:

* fabric for collage;
* making dens and shelters;
* with clips and pegs for dressing up;
* for wrapping and covering;
* for painting or spraying colour on;
* for hangings, decorations etc.

The challenge for Key Stage 1 teachers is to:

* support children in expanding the challenge and complexity of their use of fabrics;
* help children understand how fabrics are designed and made, and how colour and patterns are added.

Pause for thought

In the early stages of working with these materials it is crucial to continue to observe the children. Only by doing this can you set developmentally appropriate challenges and provocations. The ideas listed are offered as suggestions; the most exciting challenges will arise from children's own interests and motivations, which will only become apparent as you spend time with them, watching and joining them in their play. As you do this, you will be moving between the three interconnecting roles of observer, co-player, extender described below, and will be able to decide what you need to do next to take the learning forward.

The responsive adult (see page 5)

In three interconnecting roles, the responsive adult will be:

observer

* observing
* listening
* interpreting

co-player

* **modelling**
* **playing alongside**
* **offering suggestions**
* **responding sensitively**
* **initiating with care!**

extender

* discussing ideas
* sharing thinking
* modelling new skills
* asking open questions
* being an informed extender
* instigating ideas and thoughts
* supporting children as they make links in learning
* making possibilities evident
* introducing new ideas and resources
* offering challenges and provocations

Offering challenges and provocations - some ideas:

Collect samples of as many fabrics as you can find. Make sure you keep some to experiment with adn explore in scientific actvivities as well as plenty of fabric for free choice in creative and design work.

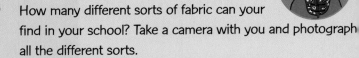

? How many different sorts of fabric can your find in your school? Take a camera with you and photograph all the different sorts.

? Can you make a fabric sample book with photos and samples of different fabrics and what they are used for?

? Find some fabrics and design and make a patchwork quilt picture. Look on the Internet for some ideas. You could sew the pieces or stick them on paper or card.

? Can you design and make one of the following:
  * a hammock for an action doll or superhero figure;
  * a cloak for a magician;
  * a flag for football or another sport;
  * a line of triangular flags of different colours.

? Find a magnifying glass and look very closely at some different sorts of fabric. What can you see? If you have a camera with a zoom, take some close-up photos of the fabrics you have chosen. Use the photos and the fabrics to make a display quiz where your friend must match the photos with the correct fabrics.

? Collect some fabric samples and try to take them apart to find out how they have been made. Draw what you find and make your drawings into a book about fabrics.

? Make a hanging with a long strip of lightweight fabric and some natural materials such as leaves, twigs, seeds and grass. Hang your creation up from a cane or dowell in your classroom or a corridor. Could you make a weatherproof version for outside?

Ready for more?

- Make a weaving loom on your classroom door. There are instructions on http://www.associatedcontent.com/article/257924/easy_weaving_for_kids_make_textile.html?cat=24 and you will need to collect some ribbon and wool.

- Now, can you make your own loom from a strong box or an old picture frame? You will need to collect all the things you need before you start.

- Can you work with some friends to find a way of making fabric waterproof? Set up an experiment to find out and test the best way to do this.

- Collect some fabric scraps and make some clothes for superhero figures, dolls or soft toys. You could turn them into other characters, or dress them for new adventures.

- Now make a bed and a room for your character and decorate it with fabrics, curtains, sheets and pillows.

- Design some new fabrics. Do these first on paper, and look for ideas in books or on *Google Images* 'fabric designs'. When you have designed your fabric, can you transfer it to real fabric, using fabric crayons, pens or paint?

- Find a way to test the stretchiness of some fabrics. You will need a friend to work with, a camera and some way of recording what you find out. What makes fabric stretchy? Can you use the Internet to find out about Lycra and elastic?

Materials, equipment suppliers, websites, books and other references

Some ideas for **resources and equipment**:

Fabric is a cheap and endlessly versatile resource. If you get a bargain length, trade with a colleague so you both get a range of sorts and textures. Try:

- asking parents and colleagues for unwanted (but clean) clothing, curtains, furnishing fabrics;
- collecting plastic, vinyl, fur and wool fabrics for added interest and experiment;
- looking in charity shops for fabrics;
- asking for samples of carpets, curtains, ends of rolls and other fabrics from furnishing stores;
- looking in haberdashery departments for remnants;
- trying fabric stalls on markets, where you might get roll ends.

Google images: 'fabric' 'fabric design' 'patterned fabric' 'sari fabric' 'woolen fabric' 'silk fabric' 'sari fabric' or 'fabric wrapping' or 'wrapped art'.

Try putting 'Christo' in Google, or Google Images to find out about an amazing artist who wraps whole buildings and landscapes in fabric. He has wrapped buildings in Germany, a whole canyon, some islands and even the trees in Central Park in New York!

Google 'fabric artists' will give you links to some really interesting artists who work in fabrics and collage, and 'fabric art display primary school' will link to some schools. Try the galleries at http://www.kidsatart.org/showcase4.php or http://www.durhamlea.org.uk/galleries and there are hundreds of others!

http://www.creative-partnerships.com/projects is the home of Creative Partnerships, an Arts Council project that supports artists working with children of all ages in schools across the country.

Books:

Angela Weaves a Dream: The Story of a Young Maya Artist; Michele Sola; Disney Press
Threads, Yarn and Fabric Projects; Marcia Riley; Stackpole Books
Sewing with Felt; Buff McAllister; Boyds Mills
Easy to Make Felt Bean Bag Toys; Jane Erthe; Dover Publications
My First Sewing Book; Cherry Palmer-Pletsch Associates

Curriculum coverage grid overleaf

Potential NC KS1 Curriculum Coverage through the provocations suggested for fabrics.

Full version of KS1 PoS on pages 69-74
Photocopiable version on page 8

Literacy

	Lit 1 speak	Lit 2 listen	Lit 3 group	Lit 4 drama	Lit 5 word	Lit 6 spell	Lit 7 text1	Lit 8 text2	Lit 9 text3	Lit10 text4	Lit11 sentence	Lit12 presentation
	1.1	2.1	3.1	4.1	5.1	6.1	7.1	8.1	9.1	10.1	11.1	12.1
	1.2	2.2	3.2	4.2	5.2	6.2	7.2	8.2	9.2	10.2	11.2	12.2

Numeracy

	Num 1 U&A	Num 2 count	Num 3 number	Num 4 calculate	Num 5 shape	Num 6 measure	Num 7 data
	1.1	2.1	3.1	4.1	5.1	6.1	7.1
	1.2	2.2	3.2	4.2	5.2	6.2	7.2

Science

	SC1 Enquiry			SC2 Life processes					SC3 Materials		SC4 Phys processes		
	Sc1.1	Sc1.2	Sc1.3	Sc2.1	Sc2.2	Sc2.3	Sc2.4	Sc2.5	Sc3.1	Sc3.2	Sc4.1	Sc4.2	Sc4.3
	1.1a	1.2a	1.3a	2.1a	2.2a	2.3a	2.4a	2.5a	3.1a	3.2a	4.1a	4.2a	4.3a
	1.1b	1.2b	1.3b	2.1b	2.2b	2.3b	2.4b	2.5b	3.1b	3.2b	4.1b	4.2b	4.3b
	1.1c	1.2c	1.3c	2.1c	2.2c	2.3c		2.5c	3.1c		4.1c	4.2c	4.3c
	1.1d				2.2d				3.1d				4.3d
					2.2e								
					2.2f								
					2.2g								

ICT

	ICT 1 finding out		ICT 2 ideas	ICT 3 reviewing	ICT 4 breadth
	1.1a	1.2a	2a	3a	4a
	1.1b	1.2b	2b	3b	4b
	1.1c	1.2c		3c	4c
		1.2d			

D&T

	D&T 1 developing	D&T 2 tool use	D&T 3 evaluating	D&T 4 materials	D&T 5 breadth
	1a	2a	3a	4a	5a
	1b	2b	3b	4b	5b
	1c	2c			5c
	1d	2d			
	1e	2e			

History

	H1 chronology	H2 events, people	H3 interpret	H4 enquire	H5 org & comm	H6 breadth
	1a	2a	3a	4a	5a	6a
	1b	2b		4b		6b
						6c
						6d

Geography

	G1.1 & G1.2 enquiry		G2 places	G3 processes	G4 environment	G5 breadth
	1.1a	1.2a	2a	3a	4a	5a
	1.1b	1.2b	2b	3b	4b	5b
	1.1c	1.2c	2c			5c
	1.1d	1.2d	2d			5d
			2e			

Music

	M1 performing	M2 composing	M3 appraising	M4 listening	M5 breadth
	1a	2a	3a	4a	5a
	1b	2b	3b	4b	5b
	1c			4c	5c
					5d

PHSE & C

	PSHEC1 conf & resp	PSHEC2 citizenship	PSHEC3 health	PSHEC4 relationships
	1a	2a	3a	4a
	1b	2b	3b	4b
	1c	2c	3c	4c
	1d	2d	3d	4d
	1e	2e	3e	4e
		2f	3f	
		2g	3g	
		2h		

Art & Design

	A&D1 ideas	A&D2 making	A&D3 evaluating	A&D4 materials	A&D5 breadth
	1a	2a	3a	4a	5a
	1b	2b	3b	4b	5b
		2c		4c	5c
					5d

PE

	PE1 devel skills	PE2 apply skills	PE3 evaluate	PE4 fitness	PE5 breadth
	1a	2a	3a	4a	5a dance
	1b	2b	3b	4b	5b games
		2c	3c		5c gym

Critical skills	Thinking Skills
problem solving	observing
decision making	classifying
critical thinking	prediction
creative thinking	making inferences
communication	problem solving
organisation	drawing conclusions
management	
leadership	

Combined Materials

Combined Materials

Previous experience in the Foundation Stage

Children's experience of combining materials will very much depend on the philosophy of the setting they have attended. If they have been to a setting which encouraged them to access materials freely they may well have had extensive opportunities to combine materials in a wide variety of different ways, such as:

* in free play indoors and outside;
* in free play in the workshop area;
* to test and explore the properties of different materials;
* when making props for role play;
* in home corner play;
* to represent objects and experiences in their own lives.

Pause for thought

In the early stages of working with these materials it is crucial to continue to observe the children. Only by doing this can you set developmentally appropriate challenges and provocations. The ideas listed here are offered as suggestions; the most exciting challenges will arise from children's own interests and motivations, which will only become apparent as you spend time with them, watching and joining them in their play. As you do this, you will be moving between the three interconnecting roles of observer, co-player, extender described below, and will be able to decide what you need to do next to take the learning forward.

The responsive adult (see page 5)

In three interconnecting roles, the responsive adult will be:

observer

* observing
* listening
* interpreting

co-player

* **modelling**
* **playing alongside**
* **offering suggestions**
* **responding sensitively**
* **initiating with care!**

extender

* discussing ideas
* sharing thinking
* modelling new skills
* asking open questions
* being an informed extender
* instigating ideas and thoughts
* supporting children as they make links in learning
* making possibilities evident
* introducing new ideas and resources
* offering challenges and provocations

Offering challenges and provocations - some ideas:

In order to get the most out of games, children first need to build up a wide repertoire of the properties and uses of different materials. Once they have done this, they can innovate and make up new versions, using their creativity to invent and expand on their knowledge.

? Can you use a combination of materials to make a character, vehicle or other type of sculpture?

? Can you make a character or structure using two, three or four different types of materials, for example, clay, wire and wood?

? Can you combine materials to make a 'set' for a story book, for example, *We're Going on a Bear Hunt*. How will you make the snow/forest/swishy grass etc.?

? Can you make a structure or sculpture using:
  * wire and clay?
  * soap and wire?
  * foam and wood?
  * other materials from your classroom?

? When you combine clay and wire, how many different ways can you find of using the wire?

? Can you make a piece of jewellery from a combination of materials?

? Look at all the pages in this book. Can you make a sculpture, an environment for a story, a vehicle or an abacus using the materials listed in this book?

? Look at the recycled resources that you have collected in your school or your class. How can you combine some of these resources with the ideas in this book to make an outdoor sculpture. Work with your friends and see if you can make:
  * a sculpture with moving parts;
  * a sculpture that makes people laugh;
  * a sculpture of a group of animals.

Ready for more?

- Can you write some ideas books about different ways to use the materials in this book, for example, *Ten Exciting Things to Make With Soap?*

- Can you use a combination of materials to make dream catchers, mobiles, Christmas or Divali decorations?

- Can you work in a group or class to make a sculpture for the wall in your hall, using a combination of the materials in this book?

- Can you find out who likes which materials best and represent the results of your survey on a graph? Ask them to tell you which materials they like using and which materials they like looking at.

- Can you make a wall hanging for your reading area or library with a combination of materials? Work in groups to try different combinations. Which works the best? Which is easiest to display?

- Can you make some lanterns using a combination of materials? Which materials would be best? How could you make your lanterns light up?

- Can you design a set of characters for a story and make them using a combination of materials? Can you turn your story into a Power Point display or a video to show to other classes?

Materials, equipment suppliers, websites, books and other references

Some ideas for **resources and equipment**:
This section is where recycled materials can really come into their own. Locate your local Children's Scrapstore by looking on www.childrensscrapstore.co.uk and using the Directory. If you have never used this service it is a great find! You can also recycle your own materials and get the children involved too. Make sure they always wash the items before they bring them to school, and get parents' permission to collect things. You could start with:

- plastic containers of all sorts;
- planks, tyres, fabrics and cable reels;
- boxes, bags and baskets;
- wire, bag ties, bubble wrap, card and paper;
- old clothes, scarves, hats etc for stuffing;
- foil containers, boxes etc.

It's important to give children plenty of time to work on their projects, providing a camera for them to record their own progress for discussions and evaluation.

Google: There are lots of sites related to recycling, for information and details of local projects. To look at some recycled art and sculpture, try **Google Images** 'recycled art' 'african recycled art'.

http://www.ecofriend.org - has a great recycled dinosaur
http://www.inhabitat.com has some cars and motor bikes.

Books:
EarthFriendly Toys: Make Toys and Games from Reusable Objects (Earth-Friendly); George Pfiffner; Jossey Bass
Cups and Cans and Paper Plates; Craft Projects from Recycled Materials; Phyllis Fiarotta; Sterling
Make Sculptures! by Kim Solga; North Light Books
Kids Create: Art and Craft Experience for 3 to 9 Year Olds; Lauri Carlson; Williamson Publishing
Art and Crafts for Kids; Australian Women's Weekly; Susan Tomnay; ACP
Children's Art and Crafts; Australian Women's Weekly; Maryanne Blacker; ACP

Curriculum coverage grid overleaf

Potential NC KS1 Curriculum Coverage through the provocations suggested for combined materials.

Literacy

	Lit 1 speak	Lit 2 listen	Lit 3 group	Lit 4 drama	Lit 5 word	Lit 6 spell	Lit 7 text1	Lit 8 text2	Lit 9 text3	Lit10 text4	Lit11 sentence	Lit12 presentation
Literacy	1.1	2.1	3.1	4.1	5.1	6.1	7.1	8.1	9.1	10.1	11.1	12.1
	1.2	2.2	3.2	4.2	5.2	6.2	7.2	8.2	9.2	10.2	11.2	12.2

Numeracy

	Num 1 U&A	Num 2 count	Num 3 number	Num 4 calculate	Num 5 shape	Num 6 measure	Num 7 data
Numeracy	1.1	2.1	3.1	4.1	5.1	6.1	7.1
	1.2	2.2	3.2	4.2	5.2	6.2	7.2

Full version of KS1 PoS on pages 69-74
Photocopiable version on page 8

Science

	SC1 Enquiry			SC2 Life processes					SC3 Materials		SC4 Phys processes		
	Sc1.1	Sc1.2	Sc1.3	Sc2.1	Sc2.2	Sc2.3	Sc2.4	Sc2.5	Sc3.1	Sc3.2	Sc4.1	Sc4.2	Sc4.3
Science	1.1a	1.2a	1.3a	2.1a	2.2a	2.3a	2.4a	2.5a	3.1a	3.2a	4.1a	4.2a	4.3a
	1.1b	1.2b	1.3b	2.1b	2.2b	2.3b	2.4b	2.5b	3.1b	3.2b	4.1b	4.2b	4.3b
	1.1c	1.2c	1.3c	2.1c	2.2c	2.3c		2.5c	3.1c		4.1c	4.2c	4.3c
	1.1d				2.2d				3.1d				4.3d
					2.2e								
					2.2f								
					2.2g								

ICT

	ICT 1 finding out	ICT 2 ideas	ICT 3 reviewing	ICT 4 breadth
ICT	1.1a 1.2a	2a	3a	4a
	1.1b 1.2b	2b	3b	4b
	1.1c 1.2c		3c	4c
	1.2d			

D&T

	D&T 1 developing	D&T 2 tool use	D&T 3 evaluating	D&T 4 materials	D&T 5 breadth
D&T	1a	2a	3a	4a	5a
	1b	2b	3b	4b	5b
	1c	2c			5c
	1d	2d			
	1e	2e			

History

	H1 chronology	H2 events, people	H3 interpret	H4 enquire	H5 org & comm	H6 breadth
History	1a	2a	3a	4a	5a	6a
	1b	2b		4b		6b
						6c
						6d

Geography

	G1.1 & G1.2 enquiry		G2 places	G3 processes	G4 environment	G5 breadth
Geography	1.1a	1.2a	2a	3a	4a	5a
	1.1b	1.2b	2b	3b	4b	5b
	1.1c	1.2c	2c			5c
	1.1d	1.2d	2d			5d
			2e			

Music

	M1 performing	M2 composing	M3 appraising	M4 listening	M5 breadth
Music	1a	2a	3a	4a	5a
	1b	2b	3b	4b	5b
	1c			4c	5c
					5d

PHSE & C

	PSHEC1 conf & resp	PSHEC2 citizenship	PSHEC3 health	PSHEC4 relationships
PHSE & C	1a	2a	3a	4a
	1b	2b	3b	4b
	1c	2c	3c	4c
	1d	2d	3d	4d
	1e	2e	3e	4e
		2f	3f	
		2g	3g	
		2h		

Art & Design

	A&D1 ideas	A&D2 making	A&D3 evaluating	A&D4 materials	A&D5 breadth
Art & Design	1a	2a	3a	4a	5a
	1b	2b	3b	4b	5b
		2c		4c	5c
					5d

PE

	PE1 devel skills	PE2 apply skills	PE3 evaluate	PE4 fitness	PE5 breadth
PE	1a	2a	3a	4a	5a dance
	1b	2b	3b	4b	5b games
		2c	3c		5c gym

Critical skills	Thinking Skills
problem solving	observing
decision making	classifying
critical thinking	prediction
creative thinking	making inferences
communication	problem solving
organisation	drawing conclusions
management	
leadership	

The following pages contain the detail for the curriculum key which appears at the end of each section of the book. The appendix consists of the following:

1. Short-hand versions of the QCA/DCSF Programme of Study for Key Stage 1 in:

        Science
        Information & Communication Technology
        Design and Technology
        History
        Geography
        Music
        Art and Design
        Physical Education

2. The suggested programme of study for Personal, Social and Health Education and Citizenship (PSHE & C)

3. The elements of the guidance for learning and teaching of Literacy and Numeracy in Years 1 and 2 (from the Primary Framework for literacy and mathematics; DfES/SureStart; Sept 2006; Ref: 02011-2006BOK-EN)

Literacy 1 speaking	Literacy 2 listening & responding	Literacy 3 group discussion & interaction	Literacy 4 drama	Literacy 5 word recognition, coding & decoding	Literacy 6 word structure & spelling	Literacy 7 understanding & interpreting texts	Literacy 8 engaging & responding to text	Literacy 9 creating and shaping texts	Literacy 10 text structure & organisation	Literacy 11 sentence structure & punctuation	Literacy 12 presentation
Year 1 Tell stories and describe incidents from their own experience in an audible voice Retell stories, ordering events using story language Interpret a text by reading aloud with some variety in pace and emphasis Experiment with & build new stores of words to communicate in different contexts	**Year 1** Listen with sustained concentration, building new stores of words in different contexts Listen to and follow instructions accurately, asking for help and clarification if necessary Listen to tapes or video and express views about how a story or information has been presented	**Year 1** Take turns to speak, listen to others' suggestions and talk about what they are going to do Ask and answer questions, make relevant contributions, offer suggestions and take turns Explain their views to others in a small group, decide how to report the group's views to the class	**Year 1** Explore familiar themes and characters through improvisation and role-play Act out their own and well-known stories, using voices for characters Discuss why they like a performance	**Year 1** Recognise & use alternative ways of pronouncing the graphemes already taught, for example, that the grapheme 'g' is pronounced differently in 'get' and 'gem'; the grapheme 'ow' is pronounced differently in 'how' & 'show' Recognise and use alternative ways of spelling the phonemes already taught, for example 'ae' ' can be spelt with 'ai', 'ay' or 'a-e'; begin to know which words contain which spelling alternatives Identify the constituent parts of two-syllable and three-syllable words to support the application of phonic knowledge and skills Recognise automatically an increasing number of familiar high frequency words Apply phonic knowledge & skills as the prime approach to reading & spelling unfamiliar words that are not completely decodable Read more challenging texts which can be decoded using their acquired phonic knowledge & skills; automatic recognition of high frequency words Read and spell phonically decodable two-syllable and three-syllable words	**Year 1** Spell new words using phonics as the prime approach Segment sounds into their constituent phonemes in order to spell them correctly Children move from spelling simple CVC words to longer words that include common diagraphs & adjacent consonants such as 'brush', 'crunch' Recognise & use alternative ways of spelling the graphemes already taught, for example that the /ae/ sound can be spelt with 'ai', 'ay' or 'a-e'; that the /ee/ sound can also be spelt as 'ea' and 'e'; & begin to know which words contain which spelling alternatives Use knowledge of common inflections in spelling, such as plurals, -ly, -er Read & spell phonically decodable 2- & 3 syllable words	**Year 1** Identify the main events and characters in stories, and find specific information in simple texts Use syntax and context when reading for meaning Make predictions showing an understanding of ideas, events and characters Recognise the main elements that shape different texts Explore the effect of patterns of language & repeated words & phrases	**Year 1** Select books for personal reading and give reasons for choices Visualise and comment on events, characters and ideas, making imaginative links to their own experiences Distinguish fiction and non-fiction texts and the different purposes for reading them	**Year 1** Independently choose what to write about, plan and follow it through Use key features of narrative in their own writing Convey information and ideas in simple non-narrative forms Find and use new and interesting words and phrases, including story language Create short simple texts on paper and on screen that combine words with images (and sounds)	**Year 1** Write chronological and non-chronological texts using simple structures Group written sentences together in chunks of meaning or subject	**Year 1** Compose and write simple sentences independently to communicate meaning Use capital letters and full stops when punctuating simple sentences	**Year 1** Write most letters, correctly formed and orientated, using a comfortable and efficient pencil grip Write with spaces between words accurately Use the space bar and keyboard to type their name & simple texts
Year 2 Speak with clarity and use appropriate intonation when reading and reciting texts Tell real and imagined stories using the conventions of familiar story language Explain ideas and processes using imaginative and adventurous vocabulary and non-verbal gestures to support communication	**Year 2** Listen to others in class, ask relevant questions and follow instructions Listen to talk by an adult, remember some specific points and identify what they have learned Respond to presentations by describing characters, repeating some highlights and commenting constructively	**Year 2** Ensure that everyone contributes, allocate tasks, and consider alternatives and reach agreement Work effectively in groups by ensuring that each group member takes a turn challenging, supporting and moving on Listen to each other's views and preferences, agree the next steps to take and identify contributions by each group member	**Year 2** Adopt appropriate roles in small or large groups and consider alternative courses of action Present part of traditional stories, their own stories or work drawn from different parts of the curriculum for members of their own class Consider how mood and atmosphere are created in live or recorded performance	**Year 2** Read independently and with increasing fluency longer and less familiar texts Spell with increasing accuracy and confidence, drawing on word recognition and knowledge of word structure, and spelling patterns Know how to tackle unfamiliar words that are not completely decodable Read and spell less common alternative graphemes including trigraphs Read high and medium frequency words independently and automatically	**Year 2** Spell with increasing accuracy and confidence, drawing on word recognition and knowledge of word structure, and spelling patterns including common inflections and use of double letters Read and spell less common alternative graphemes including trigraphs Understanding and interpreting texts	**Year 2** Draw together ideas & information from across a whole text, using simple signposts in the text Give reasons why things happen or characters change Explain organisational features of texts, including alphabetical order, layout, diagrams etc Use syntax & context to build their store of vocabulary when reading Explore how particular words are used, including words & expressions with similar meanings	**Year 2** Read whole books on their own, choosing and justifying selections Engage with books through exploring and enacting interpretations Explain their reactions to texts, commenting on important aspects	**Year 2** Draw on knowledge and experience of texts in deciding and planning what & how to write Sustain form in narrative, including use of person & time Maintain consistency in non-narrative, including purpose & tense Make adventurous word and language choices appropriate to the style and purpose of the text Select from different presentational features to suit particular writing purposes on paper & on screen	**Year 2** Use planning to establish clear sections for writing Use appropriate language to make sections hang together	**Year 2** Write simple and compound sentences and begin to use subordination in relation to time and reason Compose sentences using tense consistently (present & past) Use question marks, and use commas to separate items in a list	**Year 2** Write legibly, using upper and lower case letters appropriately within words, and observing correct spacing within and between words Form and use the four basic handwriting joins Word process short narrative and non-narrative texts

NC KS1 Programme of Study - Literacy
(revised Framework objectives)

Numeracy 1	Numeracy 2	Numeracy 3	Numeracy 4	Numeracy 5	Numeracy 6	Numeracy 7
using and applying mathematics	counting & understanding number	knowing & using number facts	calculating	understanding shape	measuring	handling data
Year 1	**Year 1**	**Year 1**	**Year 1**	**Year 1**	**Year 1**	**Year 1**
Solve problems involving counting, adding, subtracting, doubling or halving in the context of numbers, measures or money, for example to 'pay' & 'give change' **Describe a puzzle or problem** using numbers, practical materials & diagrams; use these to solve the problem & set the solution in the original context **Answer a question** by selecting and using suitable equipment, and sorting information, shapes or objects; display results using tables and pictures **Describe simple patterns** and relationships involving numbers or shapes; decide whether examples satisfy given conditions **Describe ways of solving puzzles** and problems, explaining choices and decisions orally or using pictures	**Count reliably** at least 20 objects, recognising that when rearranged the number of objects stays the same; estimate a number of objects that can be checked by counting **Compare and order numbers**, using the related vocabulary; use the equals (=) sign **Read and write numerals from 0 to 20,** then beyond; use knowledge of place value to position these numbers on a number track and number line **Say the number that is 1 more or less than any given number,** & 10 more or less for multiples of 10 **Use the vocabulary of halves and quarters** in context	**Derive and recall all pairs of numbers** with a total of 10 and addition facts for totals to at least 5; work out the corresponding subtraction facts **Count on or back in ones, twos, fives and tens** and use this knowledge to derive the multiples of 2, 5 and 10 to the tenth multiple **Recall the doubles of all numbers to at least 10**	**Relate addition to counting on**; recognise that addition can be done in any order; use practical and informal written methods to support the addition of a one-digit number or a multiple of 10 to a one-digit or two- digit number **Understand subtraction as 'take away'** and find a 'difference' by counting up; use practical and informal written methods to support the subtraction of a one-digit number from a one-digit or two-digit number and a multiple of 10 from a two- digit number **Use the vocabulary related to addition and subtraction and symbols** to describe and record addition and subtraction number sentences **Solve practical problems** that involve combining groups of 2, 5 or 10, or sharing into equal groups	**Visualise and name common 2-D shapes and 3-D solids** and describe their features; use them to make patterns, pictures & models **Identify objects that turn about a point** (e.g. scissors) or about a line (e.g. a door); recognise & make whole, half & quarter turns **Visualise & use everyday language to describe the position** of objects and direction and distance when moving them, for example when placing or moving objects on a game board	**Estimate, measure, weigh and compare objects,** choosing & using suitable uniform non-standard or standard units & measuring instruments (e.g. a lever balance, metre stick or measuring jug) **Use vocabulary related to time;** order days of the week & months; read the time to the hour & half hour	**Answer a question** by recording information in lists & tables; present outcomes using practical resources, pictures, block graphs or pictograms **Use diagrams to sort objects into groups** according to a given criterion; suggest a different criterion for grouping the same objects
Year 2	**Year 2**	**Year 2**	**Year 2**	**Year 2**	**Year 2**	**Year 2**
Solve problems involving addition, subtraction, multiplication or division in contexts of numbers, measures or pounds and pence **Identify and record the information or calculation needed to solve a puzzle or problem;** carry out the steps or calculations and check the solution in the context of the problem **Follow a line of enquiry;** answer questions by choosing and using suitable equipment and selecting, organising and presenting information in lists, tables and simple diagrams **Describe patterns and relationships** involving numbers or shapes, make predictions and test these with examples **Present solutions to puzzles and problems** in an organised way; explain decisions, methods and results in pictorial, spoken or written form, using mathematical language and number sentences	**Read and write two-digit and three-digit numbers in figures and words;** describe and extend number sequences and recognise odd and even numbers **Count up to 100 objects by grouping them and counting in tens, fives or twos;** explain what each digit in a two-digit number represents, including numbers where 0 is a place holder; partition two-digit numbers in different ways, including into multiples of 10 and 1 **Order two-digit numbers** and position them on a number line; use the greater than (>) and less than (<) signs **Estimate a number of objects;** round two-digit numbers to the nearest 10 **Find one half, one quarter and three quarters** of shapes and sets of objects	**Derive and recall all addition and subtraction facts for each number to at least 10,** all pairs with totals to 20 and all pairs of multiples of 10 with totals up to 100 **Understand that halving is the inverse of doubling** and derive and recall doubles of all numbers to 20, and the corresponding halves **Derive and recall multiplication facts for the 2, 5 and 10 times-tables** and the related division facts; recognise multiples of 2, 5 and 10 **Use knowledge of number facts and operations to estimate and check answers** to calculations	**Add or subtract mentally a one-digit number or a multiple of 10 to or from any two-digit number;** use practical and informal written methods to add and subtract two-digit numbers **Understand that subtraction is the inverse of addition and vice versa;** use this to derive and record related addition and subtraction number sentences **Represent repeated addition and arrays as multiplication,** and sharing and repeated subtraction (grouping) as division; use practical and informal written methods and related vocabulary to support multiplication and division, including calculations with remainders **Use the symbols +, -, ?, ÷ and = to** record and interpret number sentences involving all four operations; calculate the value of an unknown in a number sentence	**Visualise common 2-D shapes and 3-D solids;** identify shapes from pictures of them in different positions and orientations; sort, make and describe shapes, referring to their properties **Identify reflective symmetry in patterns and 2-D shapes** and draw lines of symmetry in shapes **Follow and give instructions** involving position, direction and movement **Recognise and use whole, half and quarter turns,** both clockwise and anticlockwise; know that a right angle represents a quarter turn	**Estimate, compare & measure lengths, weights and capacities,** choosing & using standard units (m, cm, kg, litre) & suitable measuring instruments **Read the numbered divisions on a scale,** and interpret the divisions between them (e.g. on a scale from 0 to 25 with intervals of 1 shown but only the divisions 0, 5, 10, 15 and 20 numbered); use a ruler to draw and measure lines to the nearest centimetre **Use units of time (seconds, minutes, hours, days)** and know the relationships between them; read the time to the quarter hour; identify time intervals, including those that cross the hour	**Answer a question** by collecting and recording data in lists and tables; represent the data as block graphs or pictograms to show results; use ICT to organise and present data **Use lists, tables and diagrams to sort objects;** explain choices using appropriate language, including 'not' **Programme of Study - Numeracy** (revised Framework objectives)

SC1 scientific enquiry			SC2 life processes & living things					SC3 materials and their properties		SC4 physical processes		
Sc1.1 planning	Sc1.2 ideas & evidence; collecting evidence	Sc1.3 comparing evidence	Sc2.1 life processes	Sc2.2 humans and other animals	Sc2.3 green plants	Sc2.4 variation and classification	Sc2.5 living things in their environment	Sc3.1 grouping materials	Sc3.2 changing materials	Sc4.1 electricity	Sc4.2 forces and motion	Sc4.3 light and sound
1.1a ask questions 'How?', 'Why?', 'What if'?') and decide how they might find answers to them	1.2a follow simple instructions to control the risks to themselves and to others	1.3a make simple comparisons (eg, hand span, shoe size) and identify simple patterns or associations, and try to explain it, drawing on their knowledge and understanding	2.1a differences between things that are living and things that have never been alive	2.2a recognise and compare the main external parts of the bodies of humans and other animals	2.3a recognise that plants need light and water to grow	2.4a recognise similarities and differences between themselves and others, and to treat others with sensitivity	2.5a find out about the different kinds of plants and animals in the local environment	3.1a use their senses to explore and recognise the similarities and differences between materials	3.2a find out how the shapes of objects made from some materials can be changes by some processes, including squashing, bending, twisting & stretching	4.1a about everyday appliances that use electricity	4.2a find out about, & describe the movement of, familiar things (e.g. cars going faster, slowing down, changing direction)	4.3a identify different light sources, including the Sun
1.1b use first-hand experience & simple information sources to answer questions	1.2b explore, using the senses of sight, hearing, smell, touch & taste as appropriate, & make & record observations & measurements	1.3b compare what happened with what they expected would happen, and try to explain it. Drawing on their knowledge and understanding	2.1b that animals, including humans, move, feed, grow, use their senses and reproduce	2.2b that humans and other animals need food and water to stay alive	2.3b to recognise and name the leaf, flowers, stem and root of flowering plants	2.4b group living things according to observable similarities and differences	2.5b identify similarities & differences between local environments & ways in which these affect animals & plants that are found there	3.1b sort objects into groups on the basis of their properties texture, float, hardness, transparency & whether they are magnetic or non-magnetic)	3.2b explore & describe the way some everyday materials, for example water, chocolate, bread, clay, change when they are heated or cooled	4.1b simple series circuits involving batteries, wires, bulbs and other components - eg buzzers	4.2b that both pushes and pulls are examples of forces	4.3b that darkness is the absence of light
1.1c think about what might happen before deciding what to do	1.2c communicate what happened in a variety of ways, including using ICT	1.3c review their work and explain what they did to others	2.1c relate life processes to animals and plants found in the local environment	2.2c that taking exercise and eating the right types and amounts of food help humans to keep healthy	2.3c that seeds grow into flowering plants		2.5c care for the environment	3.1c recognise and name common types of material & recognise that some of them are found naturally		4.1c how a switch can be used to break a circuit	4.2c to recognise that when things speed up, slow down or change direction, there is a cause	4.3c that there are many kinds of sound and sources of sound
1.1d Recognise when a test or comparison is unfair				2.2d about the role of drugs as medicines				3.1d find out about the uses of a variety of materials & how these are chosen for specific uses on the basis of their simple properties				4.3d that sounds travel away from sources, getting fainter as they do so, and that they are heard

2.2e
how to treat animals with care and sensitivity

2.2f
that humans and other animals can produce offspring and that these offspring grow into adults

2.2g
about the senses that enable humans and other animals to be aware of the world around them

NC KS1 Programme of Study for Key Stage 1- Science

NC KS1 Programme of Study - ICT

ICT 1		ICT 2	ICT 3	ICT 4
1.1 finding things out / 1.2 developing ideas and making things happen		exchanging and sharing information	reviewing, modifying & evaluating work as it progresses	breadth of study
1.1a gather information from a variety of sources	1.2a use text, tables, images & sound to develop their ideas	2a share their ideas by presenting information in a variety of forms	3a review what they have done to help them develop their ideas	4a work with a range of information to investigate the ways it can be presented
1.1b enter & store information in a variety of forms	1.2b select from and add to information they have	2b present their completed work effectively	3b describe the effects of their actions	4b exploring a variety of ICT tools
1.1c retrieve information that has been stored	1.2c plan & give instructions to make things happen		3c talk about what they might change in future work	4c talk about the uses of ICT inside and outside school
	1.2d try things out & explore what happens in real & imaginary instructions			

NC KS1 Programme of Study - History

H1 chronological understanding	H2 K & U of events, people & changes	H3 historical interpretation	H4 historical enquiry	H5 organisation & communication	H6 breadth of study
1a place events and objects in chronological order	2a recognise why people did things, why events happened and what happened as a result	3a identify different ways in which the past is represented	4a find out about the past from a range of sources of information	5a select from their knowledge of history and communicate it in a variety of ways	6a changes in their own lives and the way of life of their family or others around them
1b use common words and phrases relating to the passing of time (for example, before, after, a long time ago, past	2b identify differences between ways of life at different times		4b ask and answer questions about the past		6b the way of life of people in the more distant past who lived in the local area or elsewhere in Britain
					6c the lives of significant men, women and children
					6d past events from the history of Britain and the wider world

NC KS1 Programme of Study - D&T

D&T 1 developing planning & communicating ideas	D&T 2 working with tools, equipment, materials	D&T 3 evaluating processes & products	D&T 4 k & u of materials & components	D&T 5 breadth of study
1a generate ideas	2a explore sensory qualities of materials	3a talk about their ideas	4a working characteristics of materials	5a focused practical tasks
1b develop ideas	2b measure, mark out, cut and shape	3b identify improvements	4b how mechanisms can be used	5b design & make assignments
1c talk about their ideas	2c assemble, join & combine materials			5c investigate & evaluate products
1d plan what to do next	2d use simple finishing techniques			
1e communicate ideas	2e follow safe procedures			

NC KS1 Programme of Study - Geography

G1.1 & G1.2 geographical and enquiry skills		G2 knowledge & understanding of places	G3 knowledge & understanding of patterns & processes	G4 knowledge & understanding of environment	G5 breadth of study
1.1a ask geographical questions	1.2a use geographical vocabulary	2a identify & describe what places are like	3a make observations about where things are located	4a recognise changes in the environment	5a the locality of the school
1.1b observe and record	1.2b use fieldwork skills	2b identify and describe what places are	3b recognise changes in physical & human features	4b recognise how the environment may be improved & sustained	5b a contrasting locality in the UK or overseas
1.1c express their own views about people, places & environments	1.2c use globes, maps & plans at a range of scales	2c recognise how places become they way they are & how they are changing			5c study at a local scale
1.1d communicate in different ways	1.2d use secondary sources of information	2d recognise how places compare with other places			5d carry out fieldwork investigations outside the classroom
		2e recognise how places are linked to other places in the world			

73

Programme of Study for Key Stage 1 - Art & Design

A&D1 exploring & developing ideas	A&D2 investigating & making art, craft and design	A&D3 evaluating & developing work	A&D4 k & u of materials & components	A&D5 breadth of study
1a record from first hand observation, experience & imagination	2a investigate the possibilities of materials and processes	3a review what they and others have done	4a visual and tactile elements	5a exploring a range of starting points
1b ask and answer questions about the starting points for their work	2b try out tools & techniques & apply these	3b identify what they might change	4b materials & processes used in making art, craft & design	5b working on their own, and collaborating with others
	2c represent observations, ideas and feelings		4c differences & similarities in the work of artists, craftspeople & designers	5c using a range of materials and processes
				5d investigating different kinds of art, craft & design

Programme of Study for Key Stage 1 - Music

M1 performing skills	M2 composing skills	M3 responding & reviewing (appraising skills)	M4 responding & reviewing (listening skills)	M5 breadth of study
1a use their voices expressively by singing songs, chants, rhymes	2a create musical patterns	3a explore and express their ideas and feelings about music	4a listen with concentration & internalise & recall sounds	5a a range of musical activities
1b play tuned & untuned instruments	2b explore, choose & organise sounds & musical ideas	3b make improvements to their own work	4b how combined musical elements can be organised	5b responding to a range of starting points
1c rehearse and perform with others			4c how sounds can be made in different ways	5c working on their own, in groups & as a class
				5d a range of live and recorded music

Programme of Study for Key Stage 1 - PE

PE1 acquiring and developing skills	PE2 selecting and applying skills, tactics and compositional ideas	PE3 evaluating and improving performance	PE4 knowledge and understanding of fitness and health	PE5 breadth of study
1a explore basic skills, actions and ideas with increasing understanding	2a explore how to choose & apply skills and actions in sequence & in combination	3a describe what they have done	4a how important it is to be active	5a dance
1b remember & repeat simple skills & actions with increasing control	2b vary the way they perform skills by using simple tactics and movement phrases	3b observe, describe & copy what others have done	4b recognise & describe how their bodies feel during different activities	5b games
	2c apply rules and conventions for different activities	3c use what they have learnt to improve the quality and control of their work		5c gymnastics

Programme of Study for Key Stage 1 - PSHE

PSHEC1 developing confidence & responsibility & making the most of their abilities	PSHEC2 preparing to play an active role as citizens	PSHEC3 developing a healthier lifestyle	PSHEC4 developing good relationships & respecting differences
1a recognise their likes & dislikes, what is fair & unfair, what is right & wrong	2a take part in discussions with one other person and the whole class	3a make simple choices that improve their health & wellbeing	4a recognise how their behaviour affects other people
1b share their opinions on things that matter to them and their views	2b take part in a simple debate about topical issues	3b maintain personal hygiene	4b listen to other people and play and work co-operatively
1c recognise, name and deal with their feelings in a positive way	2c recognise choices they make, & the difference between right & wrong	3c how some diseases spread and can be controlled	4c identify and respect differences and similarities between people
1d think about themselves, learn from their experiences & recognise what they are good at	2d realise that people and other living things have needs, & that they have responsibilities to meet them	3d about the process of growing from young to old & how people's needs change	4d that family and friends should care for each other
1e how to set simple goals	2e that they belong to various groups & communities, such as a family	3e the names of the main parts of the body	4e that there are different types of teasing & bullying, that bullying is wrong
	2f what improves & harms their local, natural & built environments	3f that household products & medicines can be harmful	
	2g contribute to the life of the class and school	3g rules for, and ways of, keeping safe, basic road safety	
	2h realise that money comes from different sources		

Websites and resources

The following organisations and individuals have kindly given permission for photographs to be used in this book:

ASCO Educational

Web sites included in this book:

www.activityvillage.co.uk/rangoli.htm - rangoli patterns

www.accessart.org.uk/modroc.php - how to use modroc

www.allcrafts.net/dolls.htm#freeprojects - for free doll-making instructions

http://artseducation.suite101.com/article.cfm/plaster_bandage_sculpture - making plaster bandage sculptures

www.associatedcontent.com/article/133198/soap_carving_you_can_do_with_children.html - a 'how to' article

www.associatedcontent.com/article/257924/easy_weaving_for_kids_make_textile.html?cat=24 - textile art without a loom

www.childrensscrapstore.co.uk - for a directory of Scrapstores

www.bbc.co.uk/norfolk/content/image_galleries/events_ice_sculpture_20071216_gallery.shtml - for images of an ice sculpture trail

www.commotionstore.co.uk - for clay tools

www.craftmill.co.uk - modroc bandages and sheets, air drying clay, tools, shaped cutters

www.creative-partnerships.com/projects - is the home of Creative Partnerships, an Arts Council project

http://daycaredaze.wordpress.com/2007/02/14/valentine-craft/ - using grated wax

www.dltk-kids.com/World/india/mrangoli.htm - rangoli patterns

www.durhamlea.org.uk/galleries - a local gallery, and there are hundreds of others!

www.ecofriend.org - ecological site

www.forestschools.com/ - the Forest School home site

www.flyingpigs.org.uk/crafts/Soap_Carving.pdf - to download a useful pdf of instructions on soap carving

www.gladstone.stoke.gov.uk/ccm/portal/ - Stoke on Trent Museum service

www.grandeurice.com/ - and click on 'gallery' for ice sculptures

www.hitentertainment.com/artattacK/ - the Art Attack site

www.hobbycraft.co.uk/ideas_library/idea_87.html - for filling for toys and a reindeer draught stopper

www.ehow.com/ - the How-to site with instructions on how to do almost anything!

www.iamanartist.ie/clay/ - has a slide show and lots of ideas

www.icesculpture.co.uk/ - for more images, and for instructions for a glowing ice ball

http://www.inhabitat.com - has some cars and motor bikes made from recycled materials

http://jas.familyfun.go.com/arts-and-crafts?page=CraftDisplay&craftid=11565 - for how to make draught stoppers

http://fun.familyeducation.com/childrens-art-activities/sculpting/40287.html - for plaster box etching

www.jellyandblancmange.co.uk - has children's cooking equipment

www.kidsatart.org/showcase4.php - try the galleries

http://k-play.com/I_am_clay.html - for clay and malleable work pictures http://www.modroc.com/modroctips.htm - great tips for using Modroc

http://www.multihobbies.com/saltdough - has dough recipe and a gallery of dough creations

http://www.newclay.co.uk/Products.htm - for Newclay products and other clays

http://news.bbc.co.uk/1/hi/uk/800916.stm - for an article about Andy Goldswrthy's giant snowballs

www.nshima.com/2008/05/the-creative-ki.html - article on creative kids who make wire cars

www.highlightskids.com/Science/Stories/SS1105_wireCars.asp - for some children in Africa who make cars from recycled materials

www.pbase.com/qleap/mud - for some great pictures of children in the Arizona Mud Mania

http://portlandoregonweddingphotographer.wordpress.com/2008/05/19/how-to-make-a-glowing-ice-ball - a video of how to make this ice ball

www.rspb.org.uk/youth/makeanddo/activities.asp - for a download of a simple guide to the footprints of common birds and animals

http://rubyglen.com/crafts/snowman.htm - for a simple snowman doorstop

www.schoolsliaison.org.uk/kids/greecepot.htm - Birmingham Museum children's site

www.thriftyfun.com/tf957998.tip.html - for draught stoppers made from socks

www.tts-group.co.uk/ - for balsa wood, red and buff clay and tools, Modroc etc

www.warriortours.com/.../xian/0010656.htm - to look at the Terra Cotta Army

www.whiteoakschool.com/camp-creek-blog/2008/2/25/art-lesson-wire-sculpture-part-1.html - for Reggio School guidance on wire sculpture

www.workshopnetwork.co.uk/search/details.asp?Artist=355 - an artists' workshop with pictures of children making wire, soap and mud sculptures

www.wildyorkshire.co.uk/naturediary/docs/2003/5/5.html - footprints in the mud

www.vistagallery.com/html/sten_hoiland.html - for wire artists

www.yessy.com - and look for the work of Michael Wilcox

www.wire-magic.co.uk/gallery.html - is a gallery full of wire artists - click on each name for a link to the artist and their work.

NB
These websites and addresses are correct at the time of printing. Please let us know if you find other interesting sources or contacts.

Carrying on in Key Stage One

Other titles in this series include:

Construction

Sand

Water

Role Play

and

Outdoor Play

For more information look on the website

www.acblack.com/featherstone

The EYFS – Birth to Three

Little Baby Books offer lots of ideas for working with young children, and match the original birth to three framework.

A Strong Child **A Skilful Communicator** **A Competent Learner** A Healthy Child

Set 1
978-1-905019-21-2

Set 2
978-1-905019-22-9

Set 3
978-1-905019-23-6

Set 4
978-1-905019-24-3

Also available with the activities grouped according to stage.

Book 1 Heads-up Lookers & Communicators (124pp)
978-1-905019-50-2

Book 2 Sitters, Standers & Explorers (156pp)
978-1-905019-51-9

Book 3 Movers, Shakers & Players (172pp)
978-1-905019-52-6

Book 4 Walkers, Talkers & Pretenders (238pp)
978-1-905019-53-3

All the activities in these books are suitable for the EYFS. Just look for the component and age you need.

Heads-up Lookers & Communicators Stage 1: 0-8 months

Sitters, Standers & Explorers Stage 2: 8-18 months

Movers, Shakers & Players Stage 3: 18-24 months

Walkers, Talkers & Pretenders Stage 4: 24-36 months

Foundations Activity Packs

Ages 3–5

Each pack: ● pbk, resources & CD £24.99 ● 305 x 225 mm
● 48pp ● colour photographs, black and white illustrations

WINNER NLA WOW! AWARD 2004 ● era WINNER

These award-winning activity packs are bursting with resources – ideal for all adults working with children aged 3–5.

Written by Early Years practitioners and experts.

"Everything you need to plan, organise and lead activities on early years themes"
Montessori International

The resources in each pack include:
- 50+ easy-to-follow activities
- 14 photocopiable activity sheets
- 8 colour photocards
- CD of poems, songs and stories
- Giant themed display poster
- Planning chart

Celebrations
Kate Tucker
9780713668452

Opposites
Rachel Sparks Linfield
9780713662191

My School Day
Ann Montague-Smith
9780713661583

Minibeasts
Christine Moorcroft
9780713662184

Playsongs

9780713669404

 CD inside NO music reading CD performances

Livelytime Playsongs
Sheena Roberts & Rachel Fuller
Early Years practitioner/ parent resource:
- £9.99
- pbk (32pp) + CD

SILVER Award Practical Pre-School 2004

Baby's active day in songs and pictures.
A picture songbook which tells the story of a baby's day in glorious full colour and in songs with clearly described actions. Dances, peekaboo, finger and toeplays, teasers, knee bouncers and lullabies. 0–3 years

9780713669411

 CD inside NO music reading CD performances

Sleepytime Playsongs
Sheena Roberts & Rachel Fuller
Early Years practitioner/ parent resource:
- £9.99
- pbk (32pp) + CD

SILVER Award Practical Pre-School 2004

Baby's restful day in songs and pictures.
A picture songbook and CD which tells the story of baby's restful day in glorious full colour and in songs with clearly described actions. 0–3 years

9780713663716

  CD inside NO music reading CD performances

Playsongs
Early Years/practitioner/ parent resource:
- £12.99
- pbk (48pp) + CD

SILVER Award Practical Pre-School 2005

72 songs and rhymes for babies and toddlers.
The perfect musical start for the very young – fully illustrated book and CD. 0–3 years

To see our full range of books visit www.acblack.com

Continuity and progression through the EYFS

The Baby & Beyond series takes simple activities or resources and shows how they can be used with children at each of the EYFS development stages, from birth to 60+ months. Each double page spread covers one activity, so you can see the progression at a glance.

Great for the Early Years Foundation Stage!

Ideal to support progression and extend learning.

Shows how simple resources can be used by children at different ages and stages

Inspiration for planning continuous provision

Messy Play	978-1-905019-58-8
The Natural World	978-1-905019-57-1
The Sensory World	978-1-905019-60-1
Sound and Music	978-1-905019-59-5
Mark Making	978-1-905019-78-6
Construction	978-1-905019-77-9
Dolls & Soft Toys	978-1-905019-80-9
Bikes, Prams, Pushchairs	978-1-905019-76-2
Role Play	978-1-906029-02-9
Finger Play & Rhymes	978-1-906029-01-2
Dens & Shelters	978-1-906029-03-6
Food	978-1-906029-04-3

To see our full range of books visit www.acblack.com